BLIND LUK

BY

MARK SHIPLEY

Copyright © 2024 by Mark Shipley

All rights reserved. No part of this publication may be reproduced, distributed, or transmitted in any form or by any means, including photocopying, recording, or other electronic or mechanical methods, without the prior written permission of the author, except in the case of brief quotations embodied in critical reviews and certain other noncommercial uses permitted by copyright law.

ISBN: 979-8-89216-025-4 (Paperback)
        979-8-89216-026-1 (Hardback)

Library of Congress Control Number: 2024913475

BookmarcAlliance
California, USA
www.bookmarcalliance.com

Table of Contents

Introduction v

Chapter 1 Blindness and Diabetes 1

Chapter 2 Blindness and Marriage........................ 15

Chapter 3 Blindness and Finding Work................ 31

Chapter 4 Blindness and Self-Inflicted Accidents... 48

Chapter 5 Blindness and Alcohol.......................... 65

Chapter 6 Blindness and Drugs 71

Chapter 7 Blindness and Relationships................. 88

Chapter 8 Finding My Inspiration and Strength 92

About the Author... 109

Introduction

IMAGINE BEING TWENTY-TWO YEARS old, having a good job, having a driver's license with a nice car, being newly wed to a beautiful lady with three wonderful children.

Everything was perfect. Then one day, there was a loud pop in my eye, and everything started to turn red. This was the end of my life as I knew it. I have been a type 1 diabetic (dependent on insulin) since I was five and had been warned of what was going to happen if I did not take care of myself properly. Losing my sight was just the beginning of a long road of learning by trial and error.

This is a book about the true life struggles of a legally blind man trying to raise a family while fighting drug addiction, alcoholism, and ADHD, but I only knew one thing, and that was to fight for what I believed in.

Being dropped into a hole of desperation with what seems to be no hope can lead to amazing things. I prayed for strength as I learned to figure out just what it takes to be successful in a sight-driven world.

This is no easy task by any means. Try doing it with your eyes closed.

I needed to learn to overcome the fear the break through the obstacles to teach others that it does not matter what your challenge is in life because if you put your mind to it, and you really want it, then there is nothing that the human spirit cannot overcome. You have to keep trying; even if you fail, get up and do it again until you get it right.

I hope that this book can help people understand that if you have the will, you do have the ability to achieve great things.

It does not matter what other people say to you. It matters what you say to yourself.

You can do it, and don't ever believe anybody who says you can't.

My motto has always been, "If a blind guy can do it, then anybody can." There are others out in the world every day proving it. So get up, and be the one who gets it done.

Believe in yourself because sometimes there is no one else who will.

There is always someone there to back you up, even if it is only God. You can find the strength you're after if you just believe.

I have been on the bottom and worked my way to the top more than once. So join me as I share some of my experiences with you.

Remember, you are special too. So prove it, and *be that person* that you are meant to be.

Welcome to my life.

(2015)

Chapter 1

Blindness and Diabetes

I HAVE BEEN A diabetic since I was five years old. Luckily my parents were well-versed in this disease. Almost all of my grandparents, along with my sister who is two years older than me, are all diabetic. This involves a lot of blood sugar checking and insulin injecting. By the time I was fifteen, I did not care about my diabetes other than taking my shot twice a day. I was a very active teenager, and quite frankly, I just didn't think it mattered. I lived life fast and hard. I loved to fistfight and was very active in school and sports. I also loved cross-country roller-skating. This was long before Rollerblades.

If I was at home, it was to sleep, eat, or take my medicine. School for me was very easy. I was raised by my grandparents, and my dad was very _____ on me, learning all that I could. This I later realized was the cornerstone of my life. As I was growing up, my grandfather (Dad) also told me that to be the best, you had to train for it.

I had a plaque above my room that said, "The world owes you a living, but you have to work hard to collect it." I think I really took that to heart because everything that I accomplished, I tried to be the best in it. No doubts in myself of what I was doing. Ever!

Diabetes has always been my greatest challenge. Even my parents didn't know how to handle me because I just would never stop. Back then the doctors just called it extra energy, but we now know it is called ADHD. My dad had a plan. He put me to work and taught me to use that energy to expand my mind. Now since we had a great big house and just a grand woodstove to keep it warm, Dad came up with a plan. No one understood until years later.

I started chopping wood at four years old, and by the time I was six, I had a paper route. I was chopping wood and going to school full-time. I loved it and would sleep four hours per night. I still do to this day. I got stronger and smarter and faster until at eight years old, my dad had to start working rotating shifts at Crown Zellebach. So I would order the log trucks, saw them up, and split the wood while playing sports, going to school, and raising one hundred rabbits for food; for when Dad was on strike, that was something that seemed to happen more than not.

One of the many things that I was taught at a young age was if you work hard and smart, you would not ever have to go hungry or be cold. Now to get something clear, I was adopted by my grandparents at a very young age along with my diabetic older sister. She was the quite one, and I have always been the go-getter. I was reunited with my real father when I was nineteen years old, and we still stay in touch today.

My mom was asked to teach the country, and I have not seen her since I was _____. Hope you _____, Dad, Mom. I also have a half sister—same mom, different dad. Hey sis.

Evan though I had diabetes, I was never told that I could not do what I had my mind and heart set on. So in that, I cannot think of one thing that I failed at. I kept this attitude through school and pursued what I wanted without fear. My dad was a God-Fearing man, but I can remember a time when he was not. That all changed in the 1980s. He had an out-of-body experience during a heart attack, which changed our lives from that day on.

The reason that I am sharing this with you is because my dad planted a seed that has helped me from that day forward.

My dad showed me that if you believe in God and yourself, all you have to do is pray for the strength and hit it head-on. So when I lost my sight due to diabetes, I feel that I was a lot less fearful than my family. Let me share with you how it went about. My wife and I were married in the spring of 1989. She had three small children from a previous marriage. I kid you not, it was love at first sight. I was seventeen and in perfect health when we first got together. I was twenty-two when we tied the know. Just months after marriage, I felt a pop in my eye, and everything turned red. This was not a comfortable thing, not just seeing red, but feeling the pressure build as my eye filled with blood.

Now let me tell you folks: if you have diabetes, don't think it doesn't want to kill you. It may not be now or even a little later, but eventually, it will catch up to you. My job, I feel, is to write this book to not only show perseverance and hard work, along with a lot of bumps and bruises, but also keeping a light heart. If you don't let this disease win, then you can start to love a full and vibrant life with the disease right alongside you. But never let it lead, or it will put you in a hole. Don't get me wrong, it will still kill. It does not discriminate and does not care to do anything buy destroy your life.

Somehow, I found a way to allow my heart to lead the way, and even though I make my share of mistakes, I believe that I learned something from everything, and it has made me a better person. So I will share my stories with you in hopes that I may be able to help any person out there live their life just a little better and maybe even a little longer.

If you have done any crazy stuff in your life such as drugs, drinking, smoking, etc. be very careful with what you do because I have done all three and most of them for more than twenty years. I don't anymore. I have been clean and sober for almost twelve years now. I have found that I just don't know what on earth I was thinking through the years, but I'm happy I survived to tell the tale. One thing I have been able to learn is that what you do today, you will surely pay for tomorrow. This is no joke. I can only speak from experience about taking care of your body and mind before it decides to take care of you. Whatever you do, keep your heart full of love and always be ready because it turns out that was the beginning of the end.

The eye doctor told me that because of my diabetes, there were irregular blood vessels in my eyes that were bursting. All those years of doing what I wanted and not taking care of my diabetes had finally caught me up to me. Once again being my undoubting self, I told them to do whatever it takes and get me back to work so I could support my family. This was when the laser surgeries started. Within three years, I had had eight laser surgeries, two cryogenic—which is using liquid nitrogen to cauterize the irregular blood vessels—and two vitrectomies, otherwise known as Membrane Peels.

By the time I was twenty-five, I was legally blind. I should have been bushed, but I only fueled my hunger to succeed and show my children that despite the challenges, I will still be as successful as anybody else. This was the start of my unsighted and, generally, quite challenging adventures.

Every day I hear of more and more people being diagnosed with diabetes.

I have what is called type 1, which means that I must inject or be injected with insulin. Type 2 diabetes is where the pancreas does not produce the proper amount of insulin.

I really wish I could control my diabetes by eating the wrong foods, exercising, and taking the medicines prescribed by the doctors. There is one thing that I don't understand: why type 2 diabetics seem to be losing more limbs and more lives than type 1 diabetics. I have to tell you that if I had the chance to discard a disease just by trying to be healthy, I would do it in a heartbeat.

Trust me when I tell you this from the bottom of my heart. If you have type 1 or type 2 diabetes, you need to exercise. I don't mean just a little bit. You must have at least one hour of strenuous activity, whether it be aerobics, weights, or even just walking, as long as you are doing something. It might hurt you to start but not nearly as much as it's going to hurt your closest friends and family when you are prematurely gone before your time. I'm not kidding.

Diabetes is one of the number one causes of death in America. I have been at this for forty-three years and have been very lucky just to even have the chance to write this book. It has been eating at me for over ten years, and I just started running out of time. I used to think that because this was the last thing on my bucket list I made while I was in college. If I don't get this thing written soon, I may never get the chance. So if you have something inside you to do something, odds are it is your conscience or could even be your higher power trying to guide you toward you to get something done. Don't miss your chance. Listen to yourself, and odds are you won't be disappointed if you really try and go for it.

Take care of your diabetes the best you can.

This is generally controlled with a regimen of pills and proper dieting practices. There are even cases where the proper control allowed that person to regain normal activities and lifestyle without risk of more serious care, including injections of insulin. To the doctors, I am not normal because I refuse to conform to their concepts of diabetes control. This does not always go in my favor. Remember that what I may consider normal to me may not be for you. Diabetes kills, and it is nothing to take lightly. I have survived fifteen eye surgeries, lung cancer, blindness over fifty jobs, a major stroke, several smaller, almost died several times, high blood pressure; and still, to this day, I tear myself apart daily. I am in my midforties and still have all my fingers and toes. I believe the secret to a long with this horrible disease is exercise and a whole lot of self-confidence. Without these two things, and this goes for anybody, without exercise, your ability to react and adapt become lessoned along with your chances for success. Don't forget about your mind either. You got to be keen to be seen. Always be the first to ask questions and listen closely to the answers. Your mind is everything that you are.

    I believe our jobs as humans are to adapt, overcome, and teach what we've learned throughout our lives. To live is to learn, and to learn is to live. How well can we transfer? This is truly a testament to what we have gotten from our experience and time vested. Through losing my eyes, there are still things I can use with what I learned while I had eyes. Those memories are still very vivid in my mind and heart. I thank God every day that my parents (grandparents) taught me how to live with my disease at such a young age.

Whether I listed through my younger years or not, I still use what they taught me today. If you are a young person with diabetes, don't give up. However, I will warn you that not everything that they teach you is always right. We are all still individuals, and every person is different one way or another. Listen to your body because our mind is not always right either. No matter how much you learn in school, they can never prepare you fully for what life is going to throw at you.

We all think different and all have personal habits that some may think strange or some may think as normal. The point is what you choose to do and how to choose to be will only be a fraction of who you will become. So don't give up and keep that strong heart going because no matter what your age, it is still never too late to become what you dream of being. Take the positive and remember the negative so you don't do it twice. It really works. Try it.

Don't grow up too fast, but don't be slow. Just enjoy life and be who you want to be no matter what the condition. Trust me, you will get a chance to use what you have learned. If you're learning, you're living. Don't be afraid to work out. If you're moving, you're using muscles and burning calories. And not only that, but it motivates your endorphins, which is needed sometimes to jump-start your body. Once you're going, it will help to motivate you both physically and mentally. This is a serious necessity to be able to succeed at anything.

Self-confidence. You can be confident and not be bossy. However, you don't make a good boss if you are not confident in every decision you make. This, I believe, is another necessary key if you want to take on all of those who say you can't do that. Without confidence in yourself, it seems that people can pick you right out of a crowd. I'm here to tell you to not believe it, you can do it! Challenge yourself. Look in the mirror, and reassure yourself that you have no doubts, that every decision you make will be a sure one, that every chance you get to learn something constructive, you will not turn it down but take it head-on with open ears and a closed mouth.

Don't forget to be polite. If you have a question, wait your turn. People appreciate someone whose polite, confident, and willing to learn. No one likes an overbearing know-it-all. *Please* and *thank you* seem to be a dying set of words. I, for one, am a firm believer that without those two words, the road to your success will be much longer and harder to achieve. Now there is such a thing as being just a little bit too confident.

Example: When I was sixteen, I had an old motorcycle that I never learned to keep its maintenance. The clutch was fried, there were no brakes, and the throttle was stitching. I lived with my family in Oregon City, Oregon, toward the end of a dead-end street. I was confident that I had fixed the throttle problem, so I told all of my friends that I was going to take it for a test-drive before taking it to the trails in the forest. All of my friends—God bless their hearts—told me don't do it. My comment back was, "Don't worry, I know what I'm doing." So I took off.

The throttle got stuck. I panicked, and I shifted into second gear. I tried to make the corner, but a dirt bike with knob _____ on the street don't mix. I dumped the bike, and the foot peg got stuck in my left leg, dragging me down the street. So I threw the bike off me, and as luck would have it, it hit the curb, bounced back, and put a hole in my neck below my jaw that I could put my finger through.

My point is this: self-confidence is a wonderful thing, but don't let it keep you from listening to sensible advice. Take the time to think things through. It is amazing how fast time flies, and it's all kind of a blur. Just remember that if people say you can't do that, my opinion is I think that they are afraid that if you do really do it, you just might be better at it than they are.

If you think about it, you will probably grin and say, "That makes so much sense." Now I don't know about you, but when somebody says that I can't do that, it drives me to try even harder.

Never let those words go to your heart. When I was diagnosed with diabetes in 1972, the doctors told my parents that I would not live past my adolescent years. I actually visited that doctor's grave. It just seemed to me to be the right thing to do. One thing that I loved to do was fight, learn, work, and play sports. I don't recall having any fear toward trying to be the best at anything that was given for me to accomplish.

Now you're probably wondering what this has to do with blindness and diabetes. Don't let it fool you. Diabetes is dangerous and very deadly. Part of the reason that I am so _____ about my belief in my higher power is simple deduction. If it weren't for help from something that I can only feel with my heart and soul, I would be dead many times over. When you refuse to pay attention to your disease, you are taking your life into your own hands even though you may think that everything is okay. If you are not checking your blood sugar, then every breath you take could be your last.

I am building up to that.

I married my wife in March of 1989. It was what some would call an unorthodox relationship. But my family gave me the drive to never take no for an answer and to be the first one to say, "I'll do that. I have a family to support."

You may have a different perspective, but if you do not find something that gives you the drive, then you need to figure out what inspires you and start there first.

By the time I turned twenty-five, I was now labeled as legally blind and could not find a job anywhere. My children were starving. I still had months before I would start getting my social security. So I fell to the temptation and stole a mountain bike. I took it to a pawnshop and was able to feed my children. The police were at my door the very next day, and I was charged with a felony. I had many hard choices to make, and not all of them were the right ones to pick. It took me a long time to figure out that all I had to do was believe in myself and God, and the rest just seemed to slowly fall into place.

I have found that I had the most drive to succeed the more I was told it was impossible for somebody in my condition. The more I heard that, the more I tried and tried, and the better I got at hiding my unspoken challenge. I got so good at hiding my blindness that businesses would hire me just thinking that I was a klutz. Trust me when you only see a small percentage out of one side with nothing but tunnel vision; that is quite a challenge. At first I was pretty unsure about myself, but as I practiced and learned little shortcuts, the better I got at believing in myself. I learned that I was just as good as anyone else as long as I didn't have to drive.

This however does not mean that everything always went according to plan. When you inject insulin and don't check your blood sugar on a regular basis, there can be some serious side effects. Because of the severity of my eye damage, there is a lot of guesswork in play. For one, the syringes go in increments—five on one side and ten on the other with smaller increments of two in between the bigger numbers, both odd and even. Sometimes when I am in a hurry, I guess what the dose is. I have paid a heavy price for this action, and I do not recommend for anyone to try this at any time. If you cannot see to do it, then find someone who can.

I would like to talk a little bit about the consequences of low and high blood sugar or, as I call them, *reactions*. If you are on insulin, this is something that you cannot escape. I personally am very lucky to be alive, as I have pushed the limits of both ends. I can remember being homeless, just getting off work and walking into a hospital in the morning—I worked graveyard. I had pneumonia, and my blood sugar was 1,400. As you can probably imagine, they told me that I should have been in a coma and admitted me. Just before that, I had put a deposit down on an apartment. The doctors at the hospital decided to keep me until I got paid, which reassured them that I would have a home to go to. That turned out to be a very good move.

From that day forward, I promised myself and my family that we would never be on the streets again. We have not. That is just one example of many, which is the result of my refusal to check my blood sugar. Another is when I was on drugs and didn't care whether or not I needed to eat. I started feeling very faint. My wife checked my blood sugar. It was very low, which is clinically dead. What's kind of ironic is that I was standing in the kitchen with a mixing bowl full of cereal, trying to get myself to eat. The brain damage was so bad that it took three days for me to mentally recover. I should have been dead.

I know that God has a plan for me; and one part of that plan, I believe, is to write this book. The sole purpose of which is to show people that no matter what the challenges are, with faith, self-confidence, and a bit of luck, no matter who you are, if you have a dream and are really hungry enough to chase it, all things are possible and within reach.

Point to remember: Nothing comes easy. It's a lot of blood, sweat, and tears to get anywhere, especially nowadays. Don't let getting knocked down beat you up. Use that anger to feed your dream. Don't let anybody tell you what you can and can't do. That's not possible. If everyone listened to those people, we would all be robots working for them. If you have a dream, it can sometimes take a lifetime to accomplish. There is a very small percentage of people that get it right the first time. So if you fail, don't let that discourage you. We usually have to learn what not to do before we learn what to do.

God gave most of us the ability to make mistakes and learn from them. If it were not for this ability, I believe that the world would be a pretty boring place. Look around, everything you can see, feel, or smell all started with a dream and someone was inspired enough to chase it. I believe that if it weren't for all of the negativity from the people telling me what I can't do, I never would have been inspired to find out what I can.

Never give up. Keep telling yourself that you can, and if you try hard enough, you will. This is not for people with unrealistic hopes and dreams. Don't get me wrong, though, anything is possible; I try to leave the big stuff with God Almighty. Miracles are his specialty. I am just trying to help you find strength to reach your own personal goals. God bless you, and good luck.

Chapter 2

Blindness and Marriage

WE HAD NO IDEA when we got married of what was in store for us. When my wife and I went to my parents about this, they first said absolutely no. I believed in my heart that she was the one for me, and I was not taking no for a reason. Even at my young age, it never mattered what I wanted. God found a way for me to have it.

I told my friends, the first day she asked me to help her with her car battery, that she would be my wife. They all said that she's way too good-looking for me. Others said she's out of my league, but I, knowing that she was the one, had no fear at all. Apparently, I left a good impression with her to come to our New Year's Eve party. She called and asked my friends if I was going to be there. They said that I would, and she made sure she was too. I had always put my time into work and school, and when I was not doing those, I was riding my motorcycle or driving my car or even maybe fishing. She thought I was much older since I had gray hair and owned a whole lot of stuff. However, she did not know that my parents owned the house, and I was only seventeen and lived with them. But something I did or something I said sure stuck with her because she chased me down at that New Year party, grabbed me by the hand, and took me in the bathroom for the kiss of a lifetime. I was afraid that I scared her off because I put one arm around her and one under her backside and lifted her clean off the ground with a kiss of a lifetime of my own. After we kissed, she ran out of the bathroom, jumped in her car, and took off. My friends asked what I did. I said I kissed her back. She has been hooked to me ever since, along with me to her. Well, there's an oxymoron.

It is so hard to describe what my wife and I have endured through the loss of my eyes and beyond. My wife and I have been seeing each other for thirty years and about to celebrate our two years of marriage in a few days. I got to tell you that I don't know what I did to deserve the caring love of this woman, but I thank my lucky stars every day to have her in my life.

It has been no cakewalk, that's for sure. The day that my eye had its first hemorrhage, I was in my early twenties. My wife and I had gotten married. I had a good job. Things were great. However, once my eyes were hemorrhaging, they didn't stop until I was legally blind. It was so hard for my wife to take. I could not keep a job, and I did not take good care of my diabetes, which was what was causing the broken blood vessels. We, at this time, had three small children who depended on us to take care of them. So we tried that much harder to give them what they needed, despite our flaws.

I continued to pretend that I was not visually handicapped and kept on lying, saying that I was a klutz to get jobs. I think I have had over so in the last twenty-five years. Through it all, we never gave up.

I learned real fast how to adapt and overcome no matter what the obstacle. I never asked my wife to work. I felt that when I married this beautiful lady, I would always do my absolute best to take care of her and the children. I learned how to function at the top and be the best at whatever it was that I tried to do. No fear!

With that attitude, I would never admit defeat. I don't think I ever went home after losing a job until I had a new job. It did not matter what the job was. I would even lie and act like I knew what I was doing, usually walking away on top, risking my life. So I could feed my family along with our _____.

Not all of the good by any means. I now have three dozen employees, a general manager, and have been able to apply everything that I have learned. There is a piece of every job in the instructions I give. I thank God every day for the strength to endure, listen, and learn no matter what the task. To be honest, my favorite was digging holes and ditches. It's just what I liked to do. (Sorry, got lost in memories. Back to what matters: my marriage.)

I do not know how my wife ever found the strength to put up with me, but she always brought out the best and worst in everything we did. There were some years that we were best friends, and some worst enemies. I can only speak for myself, but even when we were in the middle of fighting, my heart was on fire for her. My wife was a nurse when I first met her. This, in some unsettling way, proved useful when my medical problems started acting up. She still continues to save my life to this day when my blood sugar drops on me.

Whether I can see or not, my wife is still the most beautiful woman in the world, and no one can tell me any different. Every day that I talk to her continues to renew my faith in the miracles that exist around us.

We went through twenty years of hard-core alcoholism and drug use but have been clean and sober for a little over ten years now. There were times when neither one of us should have survived. I was in and out of jail with a malicious attitude that no one could break. I had been to prison by the age of twenty-eight for taking a mountain bike and selling it to feed my children and buy another bag of dope.

We do not miss those days at all. It seems like another lifetime ago, yet I still see other people continuing to run down that road to nowhere. My wife somehow stood beside me until I finally saw the light, and then everything changed. We stopped fighting, yelling, beating each other up with nothing but bad, hurtful things, which can only be described as hell. In the end, we survived and definitely know what we don't want to be. There are so much better things out there if you would only ask God for guidance and strength to direct your attention down the path of life and not down the one of death. Despite not being able to see or function the way that I could twenty years ago, I am truly amazed at what the power of true love and faith can do for anyone who chooses to have the motivation to chase it.

There is something, however, that is concerning to me. Now as my wife and I are older, we are being told that after all that we have been through, after thirty years of being together, we must get a divorce in order for my wife to get the medical attention that she needs.

Thanks to the new medical programs, my wife cannot get any assistance, social security, or any affiliation thereof because I am on social security for my blindness. What kind of country does not allow a man's wife to get help because he is disabled as well? And unless legally separated or divorced, she cannot get help even though she has a proven disability as well. It is hard not to be frustrated by this scene of events, but we had to be strong and learn that as long as we are together, there is not anything that we can't do.

I am a risk-taker. I always have been. If someone says it can't be done, I will try until I succeed or I hurt myself to the point that I am not willing to try anymore. I have done things that most people either hear about from the news or read about in a magazine. There are some things that I don't even think there are names for.

In my last few years on this earth, I have learned that you must believe in a higher power of some kind if you want any sort of self-worth. I personally believe in God and think that he is wanting me to write this book to help those that may not exactly understand what it means to the people that seem to have to work harder at their lives just to make it from day to day, wondering if it is all worth it or just a mindless impulse to keep moving.

For those who think like the harder they try, the harder it gets to be able to try, I am here to tell you not to give up! I suppose the reason that, despite all of my adversity, I am able to be so positive is that somewhere deep inside me, I believe that if I continue to try, it will all be better one day. This motivates me to trudge forward despite the never-ending feeling of hopelessness that I know we all have felt at least one time or another.

As an example, I got a phone call from my doctor today, telling me that despite all that I have been through, they now think that I have congenital heart disease. I have always tried to never keep things from my wife, but this was one of the hardest things that I have felt that I needed to share with her.

Trust me, it takes one heck of a woman to be able to put up with me, but she still manages to get up every morning, and try to take on another day, knowing that it could always be our last. There are no words for that kind of strength. After thirty years together and despite all of our mishaps, I would not want my last days to be spent with anyone else.

If you ever get the chance remember to be honest, not just with the people around you but with yourself, strive to be better every day. Never stop learning how to function better toward those around you, and always try to remember that there is always a choice as to how we treat ourselves and each other.

I am going to be a grandfather of eight by my youngest daughter soon, and I hope that I get to meet my newest granddaughter.

I find it hard not to be overcome with joy, thinking about how excited my wife is, watching her run around, trying to get things ready for the big day. To me there is no greater feeling than to see her with the knowledge of surviving to see another of our children have another child.

I find that there is no relationship without cost. My wife and I have struggled through many battles, and I thank God every day that I still have her in my corner.

Some people say that love is dying, but I can promise you that it is still alive and well. I could probably write this entire book and never cover all of the feelings that I have for my wife and family, but then I would have to change the name of it. Maybe the next one I write will be just about my love for them.

Since I was fairly delirious from the impact of a ten-foot fall onto my head, I did not even argue. I grabbed my backpack and proceeded to walk the one-a-half mile to the bus stop and went to work. I worked graveyard at this time in downtown Portland, Oregon.

I did not understand why people kept staring at me, but I really did not have the energy to care. When I walked toward the door at work, all the employees immediately stopped what they were doing and gasped. My boss walked up to me and asked what had happened, so I told him. He chuckled, shook his head and said, "Only you, Mark."

The story did not end there. I started work at 10:00 p.m. and usually worked until 7:00 a.m., but at around 5:30 a.m., I started seeing three of everything, and I almost collapsed. My boss told me to clock out and had one of the other employees clock out as well to give me a ride to the hospital. Needless to say, I was not doing so well.

There was a hospital about two miles from where I was staying. My coworker pulled up in front of the emergency room, helped me out, and said he will be right back. He then went to his car, jumped in, and took off, leaving me standing alone, not being able to see, let alone being able to walk. Luckily, one of the security guards saw what happened, brought me a wheelchair, and got me inside where they got me straight into a CAT-scan.

The doctor walked out with a confused look and asked me if I have ever injured my head before. I of course said very sarcastically, "Which time?"

He then proceeded to tell me that my hip was bruised and that I had a major concussion. I then was released from the hospital with the normal instructions for a major head injury. I stopped at the store on the way during my two-mile walk back to where I was staying, bought three beers, got drunk, and went to sleep. Of course, none of these things were anywhere close to the instructions which I was given. I still managed to not miss any work despite the gravity of the injuries I had inflicted upon myself. This was only one of many situations that I found myself surviving, which I know that without the help of my higher power, I never would have survived. It seemed almost mechanical the way that I would wake up, go to the store, get drunk, go to work, pass out, and do it again.

Friends, jobs, and situations seemed to come and go like the alcohol that I drank, and it took many years to figure out that every time that I turned around, the one thing that never changed was the love of God and my family, forgiving and forgetting every stupid thing that I said or did with their hands outstretched, and a kick in the butt to keep me going.

Don't think for a second the _____ that the business_____ all have to learn hold ourselves up before we can walk. I say this because I have learned myself that if we do not make mistakes and learn to figure out just how you can push yourself while continuing to remain courteous and respectful enough to not have to have other people or organization help you up and out of the hole which you have dug. Please remember that language that's used along with the movements you make do matter to someone. Do remember that just because you looked in the mirror before leaving yourself, the people watching you leave are the same ones who watched you come in the room. So keep it smart, conveniently comical, and short. Make sure, however, that you dress.

Another thing that I find amazing is the fact that most drunk people somehow manage to avoid severe injury when anyone else would be severely hurt or worse.

I believe that God has a sense of humor. By this I mean that every time we, as humans, get obliterated, fall off a cliff, or run into a wall, God snickers a little. But deep down, I believe that we are allowed to survive in the hope that someday, we will learn our lesson with only enough damage to remind us of why we don't want to do that anymore. Yet we still find ourselves going back to that same demon which haunt's us. Just like Groundhogs Day; it happens over and over again, wondering if the cycle ever ends.

It took me twenty years of hardcore lesson learning, damaging both myself and many, many more around me, thinking that they could help with the constant suffering that I chose to put myself through. But I am here to tell you that there is a choice that we all can make that can and will change your life forever. When I was a young teenager, my dad introduced me to the Word of God. At that age, none of it really made a whole lot of sense. But I kept that knowledge deep inside until I finally figured out what he was trying to explain to me. When I finally asked Jesus into my heart, I felt a feeling like I had never felt before.

I soon forgot about that feeling and met people who I tried new things with. Most of them were not good or honorable. I wanted to be a part of the crowd, so I fell right in. The smoking turned into drinking that turned into drugs and before I knew it, I was taking my family on a _____ that there seemed to have no way off from. So the older I got, the more I drank, and the meaner I got. It is amazing how much we, as people, think that we are in control, when in reality, we are the furthest thing from it. I do not know how I ever kept some of my jobs, let alone some of my homes. I just kept on having this feeling deep down inside that there was something more than what I was doing.

One day I got into a horrible fight with a person that I said I loved and cared about yet had no hesitation of hurting that person. I was never quite the same after that point in time, so I got on my knees, put my hands together, and pleaded to God to take away the urge to drink. The next morning, I woke up and for the first time in as long as I could remember, I had no craving for alcohol. Day after day, the feeling was gone but was replaced with an uncanny felling to do good to other people. It took my family a long time to believe that I was done. But as the days turned to weeks, months, and years, they now know that I will never be that guy again. In so many levels, God had released me from the bondages that I had allowed to take over in my life. I now know that if you ask and truly believe, there is no demon too strong to cast out of your life if you only pray and ask for the deliverance.

I remember in my first thirty days, just putting the money that I would normally spend on alcohol into a jug, and at the end of the thirty days, I saved enough to buy a brand-new 32-inch color TV set for $234. I told you, I drank a lot. I still have and use that TV every day, and it reminds me that when you ask for the help to drop your vices, you end up with more than enough to not only help yourself but have enough to help others too.

Even though the twenty years of pain can never be brought back, all of the years of being sober are clouding the harsh memories with clean and fresh new memories with no fear. If that is not the work of God, I don't know what is. To have my children bring over my grandchildren with no fear of the past reoccurring is all the proof that I or they need to know that there is a higher power out there, willing to be there in our darkest time of need. Amen.

So if you can't handle drinking just one, and you can't seem to figure out what is wrong with your path in life, you only need to look at yourself in the mirror. Ask yourself how many people really care about you and see who answers back; they care first. I'm just betting that it is not the bottle of booze. If you are truly serious about wanting to change, then put the bottle down, pray for strength, and walk back to the ones who really care. If it is not possible, then the question should be, do you care enough, or do you need to research what it would take to make you a person worth being around?

I personally thought I was living good—drinking myself into oblivion. But once I didn't want that life anymore, that was when my life really became worth living. The people around me are no longer in fear that I may hurt them or myself not just physically but mentally as well. We all have something inside us that eats at us. Whether we admit it or not, there is a need to be more. It is funny though. The more we become comfortable in our ways, the more it seems that we miss out. Don't forget that every dream has a small piece of truth connected to it. We, as people, have the never-ending need to learn to be better by being better to those around you, and sometimes, people you don't even know.

All right, back to being blind and drinking.

One hot summer day, my family and I were sitting in front, and of course, I was drinking. A guy rolled up on what looked like a brand-new bicycle, twenty inches. So being the business man that I am, I made him an offer on it. I think I paid him $30 for it and thought that it would be a good birthday present for my son. However, still being a teenager at heart, I needed to take it for a test drive, so eighty ounces of malt liqueur later, and a "you can't _____ ride that" later, off I went.

Here's where being blind really sucks. I was moving fast with a big smile on my face, saying, "I told you I could do it." I look over the house and—*wham!*—I hit a van parked on the side of the street, and of course, being the same color as the road, I had no time to brake. I hit it head-on, flipped over the front of the van, and hit the road.

It is amazing how when you are drunk, the side effects are you think you are invincible. I didn't feel a thing until the next morning when I woke up and could not move my arm. I went to the hospital and found that I had broken my elbow. Needless to say, I sure felt the damage I had done to myself then. As for the parked van, it wasn't looking to healthy either. It seems that when I ran into it, I crushed the left quarter panel and the entire front end. I felt like such an idiot. But isn't that usually what happens after you realize what you have done the day after your drunken stupor.

Now to those of you who say that wouldn't have happened if it were me, remember that when you can't see very much, you try twice as hard to prove that you are just as good as anyone else, and when drunk, proving you are even better. Famous last words.

So just remember, if you are starting to feel like you are not good enough, strong enough, or fast enough, God gave each and every one of us our own special qualities but does not always let us know right away what that specialty may be. I have some food for thought. If you learn something new every day, then pretty soon, people will be looking to you for guidance and answers. One of my motto is "If you're learning, then you're living."

Knowledge truly is power. However, a person can still be smart and not know a single thing about life. So the secret is to be able to use what you learn. I have found that everything we learn, somewhere in life, we will find a need for what you have learned no matter how small or how totally off-the-wall stupid the answer may seem. There will always be someone, somewhere, at some moment who needs that answer. Tell me God doesn't have a sense of humor, and I will show you a world full of awesomely smart people who don't even know that they have the knowledge everywhere around them.

There really are no such things as stupid questions, only misinformed people, trying to wing it with an unsure answer that sounds good. Go ahead and try something for me. Go buy a newspaper and randomly pick out a fact. Remember it and see how long it takes before you hear that subject talked about. Now suddenly, you know the answer to what you thought was just a random piece of knowledge. Just think, if everybody learned just one random fact and shared it with someone else, just how long it would take for the world's IQ to jump a few points? Quite the concept, huh?

There are reasons we have memories, and I think the good ones are for sharing, and the bad ones to learn what not to do twice. If we all passed this information on, it would be a better self-conscious world. We all have the power to do it, and all we have to do is try. You are probably wondering why I brought this opinion up. It is because through all of my drunken antics, I learned a little bit from each one, never knowing that someday, I would be able to use them. But in one way or another, I have learned to adapt to almost any situation and how to talk to almost anyone who may need guidance in some way or another, and I am pleased to share all that I can to help.

It still amazes me that through all of my unfortunate lessons, I have not had any severe problems with my body especially my kidneys, which I test the tolerance daily. Now for those of you who came to your senses to quit being a drunk, knowing what the next day will bring, to being sober and wondering what you are going to do with all of the extra money left over that you used to give up needlessly on destroying yourself and all those that care around you, fair warning: Do not replace one vice with another. It is very easy to get cocky and start doing something else like gambling, drugs, smoking, etc.

For me it was too late for a while after quitting. I somehow learned the hard way before I finally figured out what exactly it was that I was doing wrong. I am saving that for another chapter, but trust me, it will all make sense when the book is done. Until then though, I will do my best to entertain your mind by sharing some of the hardships that I have experienced in hopes that they will open your eyes and help you understand that you can accomplish anything that your heart desires, as long as you are willing to have the self-confidence and the ability to learn and teach yourself what it takes to be that person. The way I look at it, if a blind guy can do it, anybody can. You just need to believe.

It is up to you to find out the tools that you will need, but honestly, most of us already have all of them right there inside of us. Here is where the adventure begins. One of my secret tricks is to make everything that you are trying to learn fun. It always seems that if we make learning lessons *fun*. like when we were in school, then learning just seems to come automatically. Give it a try. Make things around you stand out. Never be afraid to laugh at yourself. Believe it or not, if you make mistakes funny or turn them into jokes, they just seem easier to not make them twice.

Chapter 3

Blindness and Finding Work

When I first started losing my eyes, it was very hard to get hired especially when I always had a medical patch over one of my eyes or some sort of appointment or operation on the horizon. This presented a real problem when it came to landing a job. Luckily, God was with me on all of my prospects whether I knew it or not.

I soon learned that family and friends were the best place to earn money when it came to feeding my family. One of my most vivid of memories was when a friend of mine got ahold of me and he needed some work done that he said no one else would do for him. I told you about having no fear. Well, this is where it sort of comes into play.

We went over to his house, and before we got there, you could definitely tell that something smell rotten.

So he proceeded to tell me that something died under his house, and he would pay $50 to anyone who would drag it out from underneath his home. Living a fast-paced, young life, I figured out that your hands are always washable. This was my driving force—to suck it up and do the job. He bet me another $25 that I wouldn't do it, so I asked if he had a big black garbage bag, got on the ground, and crawled under his house.

Without going into too much detail, the dead opossum must have been there for quite a while since it wasn't moving on its own. I reached bare-handed, grabbed the body of the opossum, stuffed it in the plastic bag, scooped all the dirt and whatever was moving in the dirt, cleared it up, crawled out from under his house, and proclaimed "I don't know what everyone else's problem was." I washed my hands and collected my money, and from that day on, I became the guy that would do any job in the world to support my family. We had no clue just how far that reputation would seem to follow me.

From that point on, I put the word out to everyone what I knew, and thus began some of the unruliest and grossest jobs that any person should ever have to do. However, you never heard me complain about a single job that I did because at the end of the job, I always got paid.

Having sight or not made me the best man in the world. Sometimes though, it was not always for money. There was a man very close to me, who would usually never give me money with good reason at that point in my life. One thing though, he would always make me work my butt off for the food that I did it for.

My biological father, God bless his soul, always had work for me to do. But you could definitely tell who sired me because he always worked right beside me. Whether it was doing Grandma and Grandpa's yardwork or cleaning Dad's BBQ grill, he always made sure that I earned what I got, and what's funny about that is that I was raised by my grandparents the exact same way. Little did I know it but all that work while I was young really prepared me for what was coming.

I could never thank all of them enough for the toughness which defined me now as a man. It is a beautiful thing to see and feel those characteristics be handed down from generation to generation, and I am very proud to say that my son turned out to be just as tough as his old man. Love you, Son. He has seen and helped me do jobs that would make most people just give up. It was always a wonderful thing when my dad and son along with me would take on a project and finish it. I guess I never really appreciated it until my later years. Now it is all cherished as a long remembered memory. Through it all though, I can only appreciate what it has helped me become.

Let me tell you about another job that I took on for an excavation company. I will describe the situation from when I started the job. Me and another guy were called to the Southwest Portland, Oregon. West Hills on the way to the zoo, there is a tunnel which goes through the mountain that on top had a few mansions overlooking the city. One of these mansions was the one who made the call. It seemed that there was a broken sewer line somewhere below the house. Since it was about a fifty to sixty degree hill straight down to the tunnel, there was no way to use a ditch-witch. This meant digging three feet straight down the hill until the broken pipe was found.

There was a sidewalk halfway down the mountain that went all the way around the huge hill. I think it was a pedestrian walk or an access walkway. Either way there was no access to the break without digging. It was summertime or maybe late spring. I would_____ digging at Zan and stop at _____. Ironically, when we found the break, we had more than seventy feet and three to four feet down. To make things even worse, it was right underneath the sidewalk I mentioned earlier. Trust me, you could tell when you got close to the break. It took four more days to repair the sewer line and fill it all back in.

My hands were bleeding profusely, yet I smiled because the poor company went through three other employees as I continued to dig without complaint. As stinky and cruddy as the job was, it did not deter my spirit or my hunger to succeed. As I collected my paycheck and got a compliment from the owner, it wasn't hard to figure out that I was getting tougher and stronger. Not just physically but spiritually and emotionally as well.

So let me tell you folks, if you want to cleanse your spirit, as well as your body, grab a shovel and dig. I don't just mean a little but try digging a hole 3' by 6' by 8' in one day, which brings me to another dirty job back in my younger years right after I started going blind. As my reputation grew and as a man who would do almost anything to feed my family and I, I say almost because it did not involve hurting animals or other people otherwise the rest was fair game.

Back then I had a friend named Bob, and he and his dad had an above-below ground swine pack installing business. Bob came to me, saying I could make about $375 every three days if I could help them. I, of course, said heck yeah, never being worried about what it entailed. We all hopped in his old yellow ford and off we went. Men, was I in for a surprise. They pulled out their surveying post and camera and went to work posting flings. The pools were 35 × 20 ft. and 6–8 ft. deep. Come to find out I was the _____.

Bob Senior told me that he had heard about me from his son, and he was about to put me to the test. As he cracked a beer, he proceeded to tell me that I had one day to dig out the deep end of this pool by myself. He gave me about six hours to dig a hole that was 3' by 5' deep in the center and tapered out to the shallow end, 12' toward the opposite end of the pool. Eager for the challenge, I said, "Get a load of this."

I said a small prayer asking for strength and started digging. Fling after fling, I went deeper and wider until four-and-a-half hours later, I was done. I explained to him that my family gave me the hunger to accomplish what I did, and God gave me the strength. From that point on, he hired me for the next three summers. From there I became the worker to get. I then became known as the hungry ditch hog. From there it is unknown just how many ditches were dug. There was 1another on just shortly after that.

Right after I was released from prison, my rep I found had not gone anywhere. We were living in a duplex, and living next door was a great guy who seemed to love to give me digging jobs. This one was for a guy who had fifty rolling acres, and he refused to allow any type of machinery onto his land. He wanted 18,000 square feet of sprinkles system put in by hand. My neighbor made sure that it was me who took the job. I only had to dig down to eighteen inches with a pump every twenty feet. This went on, all the way around the 6,000 square foot house and all through the front five acres. I think that the digging went on six days per week for three-and-a-half months. Now that was a lot of shoveling. Every job I did got me stronger and smarter because in every job, there is something new to be learned.

All of this experience ended up teaching me patience and pain tolerance, as well as self-assurance and self-satisfaction. I guess I am trying to say is that all it takes is one accomplishment to set in motion the motivation that we all have inside of us. It will help you believe in yourself more and more. But if by chance, you don't succeed, don't let it get you. There are so many more open doors than there are closed ones. Plus, the world has come so far in technology that this realistically is no excuse for almost everybody, no matter what your challenge may be. Don't let people say you can't just believe in yourself. At least try until you succeed.

Do not ever take no for an answer. If you want to do something, and you believe that you can, then at least try anybody else to tell you that you can't. It won't be me, I can promise you that. To tell you the truth, it wasn't easy going blind right after getting married. Each and every job that I had, the more I learned how not to lose it. A lot of times, the job would be lost due to the company finding out either that I was blind, drunk, or on drugs. It surprised me that I was able to continue getting jobs. However, the one thing on my side was that most people couldn't keep up with me when it came to working hard.

There was this one job that I still can't believe that I talked my way into. This company built cranes, and they needed a grinder. I had a little experience handling a piece of equipment like that but I said that I did. I got hired and went to work. It surprised me, but it seemed that I was pretty good at it. The sad part though is that I lost this job due to my darned diabetes and not anything else.

I went to lunch. It was a beautiful summer day, hot and dry. I sat down in a patch of grass, and next thing I knew, I was being woken up with my final check in my face. It was pretty upsetting to say the least. At this time, there were no cell phones, and I had to walk home from where my job was. On the way, my blood sugar must have been really high because I just could not seem to wake up. Being as tired as I was, I sat down just to take a break for a minute.

It was noon or 1:00 p.m. when I got fired, and when I woke up at the covered bus stop, it was dark. This covered bus stop was not like any that you see now a days. This one was made out of wood, and unless you were looking directly into it, you would not be able to see me. It seemed that my wife and my dad (grandparent) were driving around, looking for me for hours, and probably drove by me a dozen times. When I finally got home, my wife was so relieved that she forgot to be mad. I was never so happy to be home, and I was always happy to see home.

The bad part other than losing my job and freaking my wife out was that I should've had two shots a day. The only time I checked my blood sugar was when I went to the doctor. It surprised me that I was not dead. This is a true testament to being watched over by something a lot bigger than me. There have been so many jobs but with each job came a better understanding of just who I was and what people wanted.

There was one job which taught me to pay attention to details like no other. We were living with a friend just outside of Oregon City, Oregon. My friend owned his own house and his father had a machining company which specialized in machining pneumatic cargo hooks for the shipyards of Portland, Oregon. I was just recently out of prison and in very good shape. My friend asked me how much I could bench press I told him three hundred plus pounds, and he said that would do. I did not know what he meant by that. He just said, "You'll see. Be prepared to bring all of your muscles."

When we got to the shop the next morning, I met his dad. We talked and the learning began. My friend took me over to the two-inch drill press and said welcome to your new home. I worked for a couple of months. I was taught how to sharpen drill bits, and my friend and his dad started to teach me how to run the horizontal milling machine. But my main job was to drill out the two-inch hole for the piston in the grappling hook.

Let me tell you, when the drill bits weren't sharp, the machine would let me know. It would pick me up off the ground and toss me to the side. The idea was that I would pin down a jig that held the hook with a one-and-a-half-inch steel bar. It required all 220 pounds of me pushing down on the jig as the drill bit did its job. Then I would move down the line of the drill presses, three-fourths inch to half an inch to three-eighths inch, down to a quarter inch, completing the rest of the screw holes that were required to assemble the pneumatic hook.

Every day before and after work, my friend and his dad would both take the time to give me hands-on training with the other tools in the shop. It never ceased to amaze me the amount of patience that they invested to teach me how to run the tools almost blind. Then one day, a gentleman walked into the shop and was asking for a new foot to be made for his inkwell which connected to his printer. He also requested a blueprint to be drawn up, along with the part, in case he needed to have another one made. My friend came to me and asked if I had any experience drawing up blueprints, so I told him that I had done a few while I was in college for making PC (practical chip) boards for computers as it was electronics that I took in college. My friend told me that this was my test for all the training that I had been given. He handed me some empty blueprint paper, along with the broken item and said, "Get to work."

He gave me one week to finish the project. My head was swimming in all that I had learned during the last five months of intense training. Being my cocky self, I had no fear, although I did ask a lot of questions. As I proceeded, it all started by tracing around the part on the blueprint paper then came the measurement. This was all done with calipers, which were supplied to me by paying a little bit each paycheck, so that I had my own set of micrometers to use. When the blueprint was done, I finally got down to making the part. Starting out with the wet saw, I cut off the steel bar to the appropriate size, and then it was over to the milling machine. This is where all of that training showed off.

By the end of the week, I had the new part attached that you could not tell the difference from the old one. The broken piece and the blueprint were rolled up neatly along with the bill which I wrote out personally. The man showed up and told my friend that it was the best blueprint he had ever seen drawn up and that he would continue to do business with his shop.

At the end of the day, my friend and his dad came to me and said that never in a million years did they think that I could do that on my own. I told them it was because the teachers I had were so good. We all got off work early that day and celebrated the great job that was accomplished. I learned a very valuable lesson throughout that job and that was if you take the time to really listen, you will be ready when the chips are down. I try to use that same patience every chance I get.

If you take just a little extra time out to teach, the results can be outstanding, and if you take the time to praise, the results can last a lifetime. From there my confidence was beaming, and fear was a thing of the past. After losing the job at my friends shop, another friend said that he could hook me up with a good job, but that I had to convince them that they were in need of my services.

My friend was a framing foreman for a well-known construction company. It was the beginning of fall so there was a lot of water involved. I was introduced to the owner named Greg and my friend introduced me as the hardest working laborer in the state. He then left the rest up to me. I told Greg that I was a laborer foreman and wanted $8 per hour. He said that he only hired laborers for $6 per hour. Once again I repeated myself in asking for $8 again. But along with that, I added that he could hire me for one day, and if he did not like the job I did, he could pay my wage and send me on my way.

He had fourteen laborers when I got there, and he was complaining that there was no form of organization with any of them. I told him that it could be taken care of by the end of the day. I called a meeting with all fourteen, along with Greg, and then proceeded to designate their jobs. Of course, after I introduced myself as the laborer foreman. I took six guys with me and sent the other eight to clean the yard. There was a container at the bottom of a thirty-five degree mud hill that was about 60' long. Just to get to the base of the new and growing apartment complex, the mud itself was approximately eighteen inches deep. When the container was opened, it was full of six-by-four feet, double-insulated, thermal windows.

I started off by carrying two at a time. The other guys were only willing to carry one. One is better than nothing, don't you think? By the time that lunch rolled around, I had already had four guys quit. This pushed me even harder. These were eleven of us left counting me, so I got all of us packing windows up to that ugly mud hill. By the time the day was over, ten guys had quit and the four that left told me that they had never worked that hard in their lives.

Then when clocking out, Greg approached me, and I asked him how I did. He smiled and said he never would have believed it if he hadn't seen it himself. He also gave me a dollar raise and said they're all yours. This was my first manager job since I was pretty young, only twenty-three years old. I kept that job for nine-and-a-half months until one day, Greg came swooping into a window and caught me and my crew smoking pot. Regretfully, he said he had to fire us all. I took it very hard and did not tell my wife for two days about what happened. I never did drugs at work again.

Through my younger years—midtwenties to early thirties—I may have gone to work buzzed on alcohol or high on meth, but I never, ever, ever did drugs at work again. Through my many years in the work force, it was never enough just to work, so I had learned to buy, sell, trade, and still am very good at it to this day. No matter where I was, if I overheard someone talking about selling something or looking to buy something, my brain would kick into overdrive.

    I used to have many friends show up at any hour of the day or night, and the things they brought me, I was usually able to make a buck or two on them. An uncle by marriage used to own a comic book shop, and I loved comic books. So he would sell me a case of assorted comics for $7, then of course, I would go through and pick out any really old ones or comics that I thought were cool. Then I would take the leftover ones to a pawnshop or bookstore and get anywhere from $125 to $145 for each box. Loving those deals, I bought as many as I could while still supporting my family. By the time it was all done, I had a collection of 5,600 comics for myself and my children, along with the thousands that I made doing all of those deals.

    It didn't matter what it was. If it was worth money, I was buying cheap and selling for as much as I could. This has always been something I could do ever since my dad taught me how at gun and knife show. After many years trying to perfect how to handle business, and this has been a steady course of learning when I started to apply it at my job, once I learned that just by the way that you present yourself to others, people can make the difference whether you manage a company or crew or be managed by someone else. Let me tell you about some of the more hazardous jobs that I have had through my younger years right after losing my eyes.

My cousin turned me on a job working for a chicken poultry farm. They called it *chicken pickin'*. You would have to wear professional respirator and make sure there were no open holes in my clothes. I chose to wear insulated coverable with gloves that covered my arms and duct tape wrapped around my legs over my boots.

Our job was to go into the chicken pen, which housed anywhere from 20,000 to 40,000 chicken per pen. Then we had to grab as many chickens by the legs as we could and stuff them into crates. That's not the bad part. There was as bestis, _____, and chicken poop all mixed up together on the ground of the pen. If, for some reason, you were exposed to this toxic trio, you were done. I would come home, smelling like that the whole time I worked there. I never did get that horrible smell out of my clothes or my boots. I just had to throw them away. Even this was not the worst of all of it.

There was a _____ reality to throwing chickens into crates. The reality is that when you put chickens in crates forty thousand times, they make a sound that sounds like "help," and the more you put in the cage, the louder it gets. It literally will wake you up with nightmares for weeks. No joke!

Another highly dangerous job I had was doing a job called bottom grinder. This job entailed pulling a boat from the water, letting it dry, and then wrapping the hull with thick clear plastic. Then I would take a hand-held belt-sander and proceed to grind the paint off the bottom of it to the water line. Then when done, the boat would go back to the warehouse to get any of needed repairs and then get repainted and ready for another season.

We were required to wear breathing and filtered masks, which we did. However, apparently, they were not good enough to block the microscopic particles of fiber glass from getting through. Within three days, I was coughing up blood, and I was hospitalized for the next week because of bleeding lungs from the fine fiber glass I was breathing. I vowed to never do that type of work again. I never did.

I can honestly say that I have done many things, but I have never, in my forty-two years of work, done or had anything to do with fast food. There was one job in my younger years that was probably as close to it as I ever would. I was hired at a local restaurant as a dishwasher, and it was one of the best jobs I think I ever had.

One thing that I love to do when I work, even to this day, is sing. I believe it helps me relax, and I guess, according to the people around me, I'm not too bad at it. Anyway, I worked at this job for many months, along with the rest of the crew, which was mostly Hispanic. I never missed, was never late, and was always in a good mood. I rode a bicycle to and from work, which was about ten miles each way. Then one night, as I went to get my bicycle from the storeroom, it was gone. I knew it had to be someone who worked there because it was not accessible to the public.

I got my dad to give me a ride home and then again back to work the next night. I have always been the guy who gets there an hour early. As I am waiting to start, sure enough, here comes one of the other workers riding my bike. I met him at the driveway and pulled him off the bicycle. I took it back and went straight to the manager. Believe it or not, I got fired for someone else stealing my bikes. I kept my cool, took my bike, and just left. I really liked that job at Sherri's Restaurant in Oregon City, but I refuse to concede when I was not in the wrong.

Let me tell you about when I met someone famous while I was digging holes. I have worked for so many temporary agencies that I could not even begin to count how many. I was sent out on a summer day to work for a cable company using a jackhammer, a pick, a spoon, and a banjo. I was designated to dig anchor holes to attach to the telephone poles to add stability for adding an extra line. Where I was working was right alongside a public walking end, jogging pathway on the southwest side of Portland, Oregon. I did not need the jackhammer unless I was going through concrete. Lucky for me, I was digging in dirt.

I pulled my shirt off, and I started to dig. The anchors had to go down 10 ft, so the pole was secure. The banjo was a round-tipped shovel with a ten-foot handle. So if you turn it on its side, it looked like a banjo with a long neck. The spoon looked like a really long fingernail that circled also attached to a ten-foot handle. The banjo would dig and the spoon would scoop the dirt out of the hole. Pretty high tech huh? I was on my second hole when I noticed three people jogging in all black. One was tiny and a girl, obviously, and the other two were very, very big and muscular.

They stopped and talked to me for a little bit. I did not pay much attention. I was all work. That's what they paid me for.

She stopped and talked to my boss for a little bit, and I saw her pointing at me. She said bye and jogged off. Then the next day, I was back to digging holes when they came again. She giggled as she walked up to me and said, "You really don't know who I am do you?"

Wiping the seat from my brow I smiled, and I replied, "No, should I?"

She took off her hat, and I snickered. It was Madonna. She said if I ever got tired of that job, I should let her know. I never got tired earning money for my family even if it was minimum wage. To me, it made me feel rich already. But I would be lying if I said it didn't spark my interest. I'm happy I didn't go. Love you, honey. Sorry, Madonna.

Chapter 4

Blindness and Self-Inflicted Accidents

I HAVE NEVER BEEN one to be told that I cannot do something. Now being only able to see out of the inside of a paper towel roll, you can probably imagine that I have had my share of bumps and bruises. Not ever really being afraid to try anything new has gotten me both satisfaction, as well as a whole lot of pain.

The one thing that I did not learn to do when I first started losing my eyes is to slow down. I still walk as if my sight is perfect, and to be quite frank about it, it really gets me into a lot of trouble. I would try to watch other sighted people accomplish the tasks that they chose to do, and I would say to myself that it didn't seem to tough. So I would jump in head first with no fear and convince people that I was *that guy*.

I was twenty-five years old by the time I had my thirteenth major eye surgery. It has left me with only one eye and very limited sight out of that one. Now a person can only hear that they can't do that so many times before, they either give up or go for it. I was not a quitter. I found that with enough raw determination, stubbornness, and the ability to feel no fear either to try something now or practice something old that after a while, people were trying hard to keep up with me.

It got to the point where I prided myself in outdoing anyone with good eyesight no matter what it was doing. I've done jobs that would make most men quiver in their boots. Luckily, most of the time, I couldn't see what in the heck was going on anyway. I was truly blessed that I never lost an arm, a leg, or even my head. I should have a few times to say the least.

Once most crews figured out that I was almost blind, they would challenge me by playing tricks on me like sending me down into dark apartments to tack down floors, which of course I couldn't see. I hit a lot of thumbs and fingers, but I had a secret weapon. I would bring my son back to the jobsite on the weekends. I would give him his own toolbelt and hardhat, and we would tack the floors down together. He was probably eight or nine years old at that time. He got to see firsthand dead-beating the crud out of himself, but we were both so proud when we got done.

In the fifty jobs that I have had since I lost my eyes, there is not one of them that didn't leave a scar on me somewhere. I had become so good at convincing people that I can see and that I knew what I was doing. It became a reputation. At every job that I had, I was trained so well that there was almost nothing that I could not do. After a while, even I forgot that I could not see. That was usually when I would hurt myself pretty good. So I never complained and learned to carry a lot of first aid items with me. I would _____ myself up, wrap myself up and keep going.

I thanked God every day that my wife was a CAN. I still sometimes wonder if she didn't learn all that stuff just to keep me going. I can remember, one night on my way to work, that I had to run for the bus, so I sprinted for it and shaved the right side of my ear right across a short yield sign at the bus depot. It really burned, so I knew it was bad, but I figured since I was already there, I would try to hide it. I made it about two bus stops, and I noticed it tickled the right side of my head, so I, of course, had to feel it. When I brought my head back, it was completely red, soaked with blood. No wonder the little old lady sitting across from me looked so horrified.

I rang the bell and got off the bus. I was shaking and probably in shock, so I proceeded to call my wife and told her what had happened. She grabbed the med kit and raced down to me. Came to find out, I had almost taken my ear off. So she sewed me up and off to work I went. Needless to say, work was a little surprised when they saw why I was late. To me it was just another day in my world. I am actually dealing with an accident that happened at work right now. It started off small but has ended up to be quite horrific.

At my last place of employment, I had let myself open more times than I can count. I was the general advertising manager and had my own office at the backside of a storeroom at this peculiar store. I will not name the companies because this is only about the accident that I had. There were some metal frames in the middle of the walkway which also happened to be on the way to my office. I was not allowed to touch the items because they did not belong to our company. I asked for them to be moved by the employee who was authorized to do so. He said he would take care of it. When I came out of my office, the items had not been moved so I asked again. He said he would. I came in for break and asked one more time for them to be moved. He said he would make sure of it this time.

For sure, I came into the building at lunchtime and clocked out. Assuming everything was okay, I headed straight for my office then—*kaboom!*—I smashed my foot into the metal items. I honestly thought I had broken my foot, but I went out told the guy what happened and proceeded to go back to work. Luckily, it was the end of my shift so I went home, thinking I would be fine. It just hurt really bad, but I was tough.

This was at the end of June, and I worked for another two weeks until I almost couldn't walk. But from the top of my foot, it looked fine other than being bruised really bad. However, under my foot was another story. I apparently had shoved the underside of my toe off, and it had turned to gangrene. Needless to say, they had to remove my toe and are still not done yet. Anyway, it just goes to show that being the tough guy is not always the right answer. If I hadn't been so stubborn and had my wife take a look at my toe underneath, I may have been able to keep it. Instead I chose to be a company guy and work the next two weeks. Won't do that again.

Of course, I may not be able to walk right again either. But really most of my accidents happened away from work or sometimes on my way home from work. Like one night, I got off work at 11:00 p.m. and rode the bus just up the hill from my house. Now you have got to imagine that when car lights come at me in the dark, I am totally completely blind. So I was walking down the hill toward home when a line of cars came up the hill toward me. Not being able to see, I just kept walking instead of stopping and waiting for the cars to pass. Next thing I know, I am freefalling off a rock wall. It was a very ill and strange feeling all at the same time. When I hit, I felt my wrist snap, but all that I could do was bite my lip and finish walking home.

When I got there, we had company from out of town. I didn't want to be rude, so I stayed up and visited with my friend, even though my wrist was swollen and black and blue. The next day, I went to the hospital and found that my wrist was broken.

One time I was on my way to pick up my paycheck at my brand-new job that I had only for about six weeks. I got off the bus across the street from work, walked over to the corner, pushed the button, and when the light turned green, I stepped off the curb and proceeded to disintegrate the platform that my kneecap stood on. Needless to say, I had to be dragged across the street where I called the ambulance and then my wife. The thing that amazed me was that my wife was on the other side of town. I was a quarter mile away from the ER and my wife beat the ambulance there.

Now it was really awesome that work saved my job for thirteen weeks and then my first day back to work I stepped in a hole and rebroke my leg. I told you I was hard on my body. I remember one day my boss gave me a ride home. We had worked all night and was in the middle of a conversation when, all of a sudden, my right side went numb, and I fell over even though I was still trying to talk. It turns out that even though I was thirty-three years old, I could still have a major stroke. It took two and a half months to regain the use of my right side only because I had bought a new guitar the day before and had not gotten to play it. I was not going to let the stroke win. I still play to this day.

There isn't a day that goes by that I don't bang, bump, or ram my head into at least one thing. I've always said that God has a sense of humor because he gave me an indestructible body and bad eyes, and he giggles every time I bounce off something. I must admit that I giggle a little too because if you can't laugh at yourself, sometimes it is hard to truly find humor in other things.

I remember one night when we did not have a home, but I had rented a motel for a week with a part of my work wages. My wife and I had run out of cigarettes. It was about a quarter-of-a-mile walk to the convenience store, so off I went. Now this particular stretch of road had no streetlights at all, so it was very dark. I actually had to keep looking down at the white lines for the bike lane just so I could make sure I was not in the street. Way up ahead of me, I just could barely make out a small bouncing light.

I did not think much of it other than it was ahead of me. It was about 3:00 a.m., so there were really no cars on the road, yet still that tiny little bouncing light seemed to rapidly get a bit bigger. I was dressed all in black with my big south pole winter jacket and black slacks and shoes. I did have my blind cane though and was using it. I thought I heard a slight noise ahead of me but could see absolutely nothing, and still that little bouncing light drew nearer, when all of a sudden—*wham!*—I was hit head-on. It knocked me right onto my butt. I tried to let my one eye adjust, and I had a splitting headache. Then I heard movement beside me. It seems that the little bouncing light has a guy flying down the dark road on his bicycle. We both hit each other so hard that it broke his bike clean in half. I picked myself up and tried to pull him from the center of the road. He started to become very angry, but then apparently noticed the blind cane. He apologized and so did I.

I felt so bad for him because not only was he messed up but so was his bicycle. He's been a tough one to hold me for a long time. If that guy ever gets a chance to read my book, I just want to say that I am truly sorry for what transpired that night, and I hope you can find it in your heart to forgive me. This situation brings to mind another memory that has to do with the wheels.

In my early midtwenties was when the surgeries got pretty hot and heavy because my blood vessels in my eyes would not stop hemorrhaging. So the first thing to do was to check my ability to see at night, as well as out the sides of my eyes.

Back then it was hard for me to find work because of all the eye surgeries. So my family and I lived with my parents until things smoothed out. At that time, there were two things that I could not love without, not counting my family, of course. Anyway, the two things were alcohol and pot. I had traded a quarter pound of pot to a friend of mine for a 1985 Honda Spree scooter. It was only 50 cc but a lot of fun to drive. So one night, I figured that I would ride my scooter over to a friend's house to get some pot from him. Now during the day, it was a straight shot to his house, but remember at night, I could barely see anything.

So I gave my wife a kiss. She wished me luck and off I went. I made it through the first half fairly easy because of all the streetlights, but the second half was the challenges. There were no streetlights at all, and my friend was at the very end of it. So I took off without a drop of fear, then the traffic started to honk at me, and as I looked down, I was driving down the wrong side of the road. So I pulled over and let all the cars pass, and then I was back on the road again.

Then came my second problem—seeing the street that I needed to turn down. I was doing about twenty-five miles per hour when I took the left turn. It was a long lulling corner which I was not used to at night. I went through the neighbor's lawn, taking out his mailbox, along with a couple of yard ornaments. I picked myself up, got off of his lawn, and tried to put everything back as best as I could. That poor mailbox didn't make it through. When I got to my buddy's house, I was all torn up and bleeding. He asked what happened, and I told him. We both had a good laugh. He told me I was crazy, and then back on my way I went.

I used to ride my mountain bike back and forth to work until one day, I was cruising along at about twenty miles per hour, and this telephone pole just jumped out of nowhere and hit me. Now what was so funny this was when was I hit, I landed on my feet, but the bike kept on going. It messed it up pretty good too, I must say. So I straightened the handlebars the best that I could and continued on to work.

It didn't matter where I was going or what I was doing. I always managed to find a way to mess myself up. Every year my wife and I would go to the Pacific Coast to a place called Barview Jedi at the beginning of August to celebrate our youngest daughter's birthday a couple of years ago. We were following a line of tourists to see the ocean. There was only one rock in the middle of the dune. I, of course, I didn't see it, fell over it, and busted myself wide open. Everyone got a laugh out of it because there was only one rock in the whole giant dune. Once again my loving wife pulled out the first aid kit, cleaned me up, and off we went like nothing happened.

Now as for minor injuries, those are something that I have learned to roll with many years ago. I think that if you put yourself in my shoes, you may find some of these kind of funny. But first, I would like for you to try an experiment for me. Take an empty toilet paper roll and put it up to your left eye. Then take something dark and cover your right eye completely. Welcome to my world. Next, be a sport and start walking around. I would like to share, as close as I can, exactly what it is like for me. Now imagine no depth perception and color blindness. Go outside and picture that you can't tell the difference between the sidewalk and the street. To me they look the same. Which brings to light my first funny thing that has been a daily thing for me—curbs and crosswalk ramps.

I trip over a curb at least twice a day at those funny little ramps at the corners of sidewalks that are not ever quite even with the road. I have tripped, twisted, face-planted, and fallen more times than I could ever count. Just like uneven sidewalks, there's another one that is absolutely unforgiving. Now keep that stuff over your eyes because we are just getting started.

Tree branches are God's attention-getters. I have bloodied my face up so bad before from trying to take a shortcut that people would stop and ask if I saw the person who beat me up. All I could do was laugh. Here's a memory you will really get a trick out of. I was an assistant manager for a 76 Gas Station. There were only two islands, and the pumps were old-fashioned, not like those digital ones, which, for me, are really hard to see. So on a summer day, I was torn between the islands and doing my job when, all of a sudden, this woman comes flying into the station way too fast. I did not see her coming, but I sure felt it when she hit me and sent me falling across the parking lot.

Being the good employee that I was, I brushed myself off, ran up to greet her, and asked her if I could help her. The other people at the station just watched in amazement that I did not get angry. She then asked if I would take a check, so I proceeded to point to a sign that said "No Checks." She got so angry at me because I would not take a check that she said she should have killed me when she hit me and almost hit me again on her way out.

I got to tell you, it really does hurt when you're hit by a big Ford F-250 and have no clue that it's coming. Needless to say, I decided to take a break. Tell me God's not watching out for me. I know he is and will never doubt it for a second.

I got to tell you that glass doors have definitely got it in for me. It never seemed to fail when I get to downtown Portland, Oregon. Almost every building has great big glass doors. All it takes is for someone to open a glass door and me to trip over on one of those uneven sidewalks, and you expect a head-banging accident. It amazes me how often it really does seem to happen to me. I must admit that it is pretty dog gone funny for me just to navigate myself to the grocery store.

You have got to picture a 260-pound guy with a patch over his right eye and only being able to see out the radius of a toilet paper roll with a great big smile on his face. However, it never failed that it seemed like I can't help but run into at least one person or knock over at least one display. I do get what I was after though, with absolutely no fear. The trick is to know exactly what it is that you are after. I would be lying if I told you that once in a while, I get side tracked.

Though I am generally a simple guy, I am also kind of like a caveman. If it is shiny or makes a lot of noise, I surely become interested in it. I love survival stuff especially something with a sharp blade or point on it. Sounds kind of dangerous, doesn't it? Like I said it is still hard for me to accept that I am pretty much blind.

Okay, now picture a person in the store, going down each aisle, doing Mach one with no regard for anyone else. You know the one; they fly through the aisles, always looking straight forward, never slowing down, and never saying excuse me. These people, for some reason, got my number. It seemed that while I was directing my sight to the items that I was after, the super speed shopper was _____ up for a head-on crash. What really sucked was when this person hit me was the thoughtlessness to fly to turn the table away from themselves, and looked at me as If I should apologize when it was them who hit me. Most people would probably get angry but once again, karma works in mysterious ways, so I apologized and move on.

Life is just too short. There is one self-inflicted incident that I really don't talk too much about. I smoked cigarettes for twenty-six and a half years, and by the time I was in my late twenties, I was getting pneumonia every winter/spring. I, of course, couldn't blame it on my stubbornness and smoking, so I would just take the cough syrup and antibiotics, always saying that the fault lay on the weather but never on the smoking.

Then in 2007, my wife and I were visiting her mother, and my lungs were so bad that sleeping was only done sitting up. By morning even sleeping in the recliner wasn't working. My wife called an ambulance because I couldn't walk without wanting to throw up or pass out. So they hooked me up to the oxygen monitor, and off we went to the hospital. Halfway there I was starting not being able to breathe. Then all of a sudden, my oxygen intake dropped to zero. Then the attendant's attention turned to keeping me alive and not just giving me a ride. He took the air tube and pushed it past whatever was blocking my airflow. They figured it was the phlegm from the pneumonia that had blocked my air way, so they managed to stabilize my breathing, and at this point, we were in a much bigger hurry than when we had started.

They were ready when we got there with IV antibiotics and all kinds of life support machines. After a couple of days of intensive testing, they attributed my breathing stopping to the infection I had. They sent me home with a bucket of medicine. In the x-rays, what they called phlegm looked like big blobs on the film, but two weeks later, the blobs were not gone.

Then came the biopsies. If you have never had one, trust me, you don't want one. Talk about uncomfortable, man, oh man! The test was so risky that they gave me percentage rates. Luckily the odds were in my favor. We said a prayer and they put me under. By the end of the day, I was back home, under the impression that I would have the results in two to three days. Nine days later, my wife and I were working in the front yard when the call came in. I didn't even have to say anything to my wife when I got the news. I had a highly malignant tumor in my right lung. All I knew as that lung cancer wasn't no joke.

My wife fell into tears just by the look on my face. I am not one to give up though. So I asked the doctor about what we could do. He asked how soon I could be at the hospital to operate. I said the following morning, and at 6:00 a.m. I was under the knife. They could not spread my ribs, so they cut three of them out. But get this, they could only fit two back, so they staggard two back in to plug the hole, and with some staples and wire mesh, they covered up the hole. Oh yeah. They ended up taking the lower lobe of my right lung clean out with nine staples and dozens of stitches. Needless to say, that tickled a little bit.

Now talk about a glutton for punishment. Even after the surgery, I did not quit smoking except for the days it took me to heal. If I hadn't choked on the tumor in my windpipe, I would already be dead, but I believe that God had that happen that way for a reason. It seems to come easy to me now to be nice to others and thank God every day that I am still alive. That's what I would consider a real God shot. Thank you, Lord.

Something else that seemed a little odd to me was that my grandfather on my mother's side died of the same kind of cancer and apparently it only attacks the internal organ. By the time they found it in him, it was too late. So I believe it really was divine intervention. I have been through so many accidents that it is hard to pick out which ones can't really get across what it is that I am trying to point out not to do. I can say slow down and pay attention to what is all around you. Smell the different scents in the air because they also can give you warnings of what is around you. Use your ears to listen because you cannot always trust what your eyes tell you. Pay attention to your feelings.

I am a firm believer in listening to your sixth sense. Your senses will work in unison with you if you just pay attention. Now feeling with your mind is different than feeling with your body. Let's try a test. Take a chain, set of keys, or something that jingles kind of loud. Blindfold your eyes, but before you do that, find an open room where the sound will echo off the walls. Then use blindfold, throw the item you chose to make a lot of noise and open your ears. Use your mind to help you picture where the item landed. If you went right to it the first time, pick it up and continue to throw it farther away from where you are standing. This will help train your brain to depend on something other than your eyes.

Try closing your eyes or cover them and walk into different areas that are first familiar to you and then unfamiliar to you. Remember the difference in sound. These exercises will help you to understand how not to be dependent on some of your other senses. Pay attention to them, then try doing it with different senses—cover your eyes and plug your ears and repeat the same discipline only with all different kinds of things. After practicing these things, you will become attuned to what your body and brain are telling you. Whether or not you have a disability or challenges, doing these things will help you feel empathy for those who cannot perform these tasks with the help of their other senses.

I'm just betting the next time that you see someone with a blind cane or using sign language, you will have a better understanding of what that person is going through. This seems to be especially hard for the younger generation, and that is nobody's fault but our own. We all should be showing our children how to help and adapt to people with special needs.

Speaking of that, I have one more story to tell you about before I am finished with this chapter. Not too long ago, I was in my wheelchair and had taken the MAX Train down to my attorney's office in Downtown Portland. You will have to picture a kind of train depot between First and Second streets. My attorney was on Second Street. There are poles across both sides of Second Street so that no cars can go through due to the train. To me each side of the road looked the same. So I was looking along and decided to take the east side of the street, and next thing I know, I ran right off the ramp onto the train tracks. I was stuck when, out of nowhere, five or six guys jumped onto the tracks and took ahold of my chair and lifted me eighteen inches back onto the ramp. I cannot thank them enough because if they didn't see me fall off the edge, I could have very will have been a MAX Train ornament.

Anyway, I never did that mistake twice. All I am saying is everyone has the ability to be a hero, so pay close attention and never hesitate to give a helping hand because you might be that persons only chance for life.

Be safe keep your faith. Be strong; you can't go wrong. And most of all, have no fear when someone's end could be near. Thanks for listening.

Chapter 5

Blindness and Alcohol

WHERE DO I START? I guess I'll start at the beginning. When I was about 15 years old, I was 511, weighed a 190 pounds, and had a full beer and started drinking beer with my friends and buying it for them. And that wasn't so bad.

It was only recreational. But from there, as I got older and I anticipated being old enough to drink, which in my state is 21 years old, I really got excited about this. In between work and school and everything else, I always seem to find time to have a drink or at least twice a week. But as I got older and life became more free for me, even though I always worked, it was easier for me to drink. And it just seemed to be second nature as my father was a hardcore alcoholic. When I turned 21 was when the drinking really really started and I gotta tell you, I really enjoyed drinking, but I really was not a very good drunk.

I always thought that it was somebody else's fault that I would get angry until when I quit. Everything just seemed to stop and get better. Coming to find out, as I look back now, it really was not anybody else other than me, which is a terrible thing because I never could admit that to myself. I got in a lot of trouble drinking and being drunk. I hurt all the people around me, including my family, my children, my parents, my grandparents, anyone that was around me, were either devastated or hurt terribly by my actions being drunk or on drugs or both.

I finally quit in 2003, and everything became amazing from that point. No longer did the fighting go on. No longer was all the actions of the guy that I was doing alcohol, especially being blind, which created its own problems. Just drinking and being blind in itself I had fallen in a 10 foot empty swimming pool, was unconscious for 2 and a half hours, and crawled out of it, was all tore up, walked to work, and had a major concussion on the back of my head from landing head first in the swimming pool all because I'd gotten drunk on tequila before I went to use a friend's bathroom and forgot the pool was there because I was so drunk.

And I just walked right off the edge and fell right into the 10 foot deep swimming pool. Kind of crazy. Lucky I survived. However, that's only one of many, many, many things that I had done just crazy being inebriated. But the most important thing about having visual impairment and drinking is you should never do it.

It alters your perception, and the more you drink, the more honorary you get, and you think you're indestructible when little do you realize you're destroying everything and everyone around you. And at that point, you just don't care. How horrible of me, period. Me and my wife, we fought like cats and dogs every time we'd get drunk or use drugs, and I have no one to blame for that but myself. And I still hurt to this day for all the heartache that I caused in doing those actions during that time.

I hope someday they're able to forgive me and and accept the fact that I have changed to try to make my life better. And it did get continuously better. When I wrote this book, I had been clean and sober for 12 years. I'm very proud of myself. And if it were not for the will of God to help me to get through this. I prayed for deliverance, and the next day I woke up and it was gone. I never had an urge. I never wanted to drink. I never wanted to do drugs. I never not wanted to do any of it.

All of a sudden, life was just beautiful. So for those people out there who's having problems, try looking to your higher power and asking for deliverance from the burden of carrying that around. And you will get delivered if you truly want to quit and you believe that you want to quit. I've been in jail dozens and dozens of times because of my drinking and excessive drug use, and I'm truly ashamed as I look back of all the horrible things I've done and all the terrible things I've done to people while I was drunk or on drugs or both, including working. I'd show up at work drunk, and I would work multiple jobs being legally blind.

I never had any fear and never had a problem going and getting jobs to try and support my children. But the problem was when I got done, all I would do is stop and get beer on the way, drink those before I got home, and it was just horrible to take that home to my family. And I'm so sorry every day for that. I cannot turn back time, but I'm talking about this because I'm hoping maybe I can help some of you out there make the right decisions to not do it. Like I said, I love drinking, but I was a horrible drunk.

And I had no problem having an inverted fuse and exploding anytime I got an altercation. Just absolutely horrific. As some examples, I could drink 8 shots of tequila, and I'd be happy happy. If I drank a night, it would be like flipping a light switch, and I would turn into somebody different that you never wanted to be around. I was obstinate, and I was angry, and I was violent, and I never backed down.

And those are horrible traits when you're trying to raise a family like me and my wife were. It was terrible for my children to see that, and there's nothing I can do to take back that time other than change and try to make it better. I know they will probably never forgive me for that time. All I can do is ask for forgiveness now, and please be thankful that we all made it through it as we did. I love my family, and I love everyone around me that I care about.

And I want the world to know that it's really not that hard to change. All you have to do is want to do it. And I'm hoping to inspire other people to continue to make change and make the world a better place, one book at a time. All I know is a family member of mine and I got in a fight one night. We were watching a TV commercial before I went to work to work graveyard, and I had drank a whole bunch of beer.

And we got in a fight over the color of a t-shirt of the stripes of a girl on a commercial, and it ended up getting into a fist fight. And I hurt that person horribly, and that was the last time I drank. And I promised I would never do it again. And at this point, in 2015, I have kept my promise. It has been 12 years, and I don't plan on doing it again.

Although I do not know what the future holds, all I know is I have control over who I am, and we need, as people, to take control over who we are and make the proper decisions that affect everyone around us. If not for the inspiration of God, I would have never ever quit, and my life would have never gotten better and never changed. So a word of advice for someone out there who has physical or mental problems and think that they need to depend on alcohol or drugs. Don't do it. It's so much better without it, and you don't really realize it until you are without it.

And everything just amazingly gets better. There was no more fighting. I started having wonderful things and a wonderful life after all that disappeared. And like I said, I always thought it was somebody else. But after I stopped, it was amazing to look back and realize the one who I thought it was was myself as I look in the mirror.

It just took too long for me to admit that, and the damage that's been done has been devastating. But I'm hoping that other people can learn from this. And please, if you knew me or know me, please forgive me if I hurt you or in any way offended you. That was not the real me. I love everyone around me, and I'd love to spread that world and positive influence to the rest of the world in hopes that it'll start one person at a time to make a change.

And if I can change one person's life by reading these chapters, then I feel my job is done. Other than that, it's all food for thought, and please search your heart. And if you feel you need change, then strive to make those strong changes and stick to them. And you'll be amazed how much of a difference it'll make in not just your life, but the lives around you.

I guess that's all I have to say about this chapter. And still working to recover and build back up the lost good times that we had because of my terrible drinking and drug use. But that's gone now, and I don't miss it. I'll guarantee you.

Chapter 6

Blindness and Drugs

THIS CHAPTER IS GOING to start off a little weird.

When I was seventeen years old, I did my first line of methamphetamines. I put it up my nose. Little did I know that one line of that drug started a never ending roller coaster ride that cost me almost twenty years, hundreds and thousands of dollars, not to mention my relationships with all who I loved around me and the heart that I once had inside me. When I was in college, I had dreams and goals which were supposed to encourage me to do and be the best that was humanly possible. But when I put that line in my nose. Time just seemed to stop.

The one thing that I did still manage to keep doing was work. And when I could go absolutely as fast as humanly possible. It just amazes me that I never killed or harmed anyone other than myself during this time.

Things seemed to go okay until I started losing my eyes due to the massive drug and alcohol overuse, which I thought was harmless and fun in the beginning. Believe it or not, it took the most vibrant years of my life and stomped them into the ground. I did not think that I could ever escape the grip that the drugs had on me and my life. But in the end, all I ever needed to do was just ask for the strength to face my demons that weren't that powerful after all.

By the end of this chapter, I will explain exactly what I meant by that and hopefully you will relate with me a little better. Now once I figured out that I could work more than one job, I came to the conclusion that as long as I tried to pay the bills, such as rent, electricity, and so on, then the extra money could be spent on more drugs. I got a story for that one that I think will make your jaw drop while you say, "What the heck is wrong with you."

I can remember a time when I was working two full-time jobs and was still not good enough to keep my family and I from living on a riverbank of Williamite River for six months. This was not because I did not make enough money, but was because no one would rent to us. The money was never the problem. It seemed that prior to that moment, everywhere we moved to there was always one conflict or another. Be it us against a neighbor, against the owner/manager or just us against ourselves. Either way, we always ended up in a courthouse. That time was our third FED (Final Eviction Decree). We paid six months in advance on our rent but did so many drugs and drank so much that the fighting, I guess, just became a regular routine that we just couldn't stop. I just could not stop.

I do not wish for anyone to ever think that for a second, I could not have made it all stop. Somewhere deep inside, I just was not ready. So we would spend a half or two-thirds of our time in tents until I got paid, and then we would rent a motel room for a few days to a week. I will share with you just a little bit of how sneaky I just really was. Now at this time, I was in my late twenties, and I had been to prison but still refused to stop drinking and doing drugs.

One night when my wife, our kid, and I were staying at a motel located right side of the Williamite River, we had misplaced a door key. I went back to the main counter, explained what happened, and got a spare key. Somehow later that night, we found the original door key. I suppose when the time came to check out, I had neglected to mention the spare key, I suppose. Anyway, throughout our time living on the riverbank, twice a week, we would produce that spare key, sneak up to the room, which I would knock on first. We would all go inside, take shower, watch some TV, even give our dogs baths, and then leave a pile of dirty towels and sneak back out.

I often wondered what the cleaning crew thought when they got a call that the room needed cleaning even though the crew left the room spotless. I often think about that and know that God was watching out for us and contributed it to him wanting us to be clean. We never were caught even after six months.

I finally got a nice little old lady to believe in me, and she rented my wife and I a small studio apartment so we could be off the streets. If I just would have quit doing the meth, I would have never been there to begin with. This is a hard lesson to learn when you are young and think that you know it all. I must say that the absolute hardest part of me was when I was awake for more than twenty-four hours.

Everything seemed to change for the worst. Being mostly blind would cause severe apparitions in reality. Some people would call this a case of the meth monsters. This is when your brain cannot decipher what it is your seeing or hearing. For me it was like looking through a wavy fish tank, and you would swear that there was always someone following you or talking about you. After some time, two or three days of this, I would start to question my own sanity. There were even times when friends or family would play tricks on me like flashing lights through the dark or whispering in the dark. That was the worst.

I can look back now and laugh at what an idiot I was for ever doing drugs, but at that time, all I could do was survive. I still had no clue how I was able to function at my workplace. Sometimes I would be high. Other times I would be drunk. Sometimes I would be both, but it always seemed that I could function good enough to not get caught. The only one that I can thank for that was my higher power because without that strength, it should have been impossible. I don't believe that God ever stopped looking out for me.

I think I just stopped remembering to think about what he wanted for me. I can remember times when I was walking home. My sight was so foggy from being up so long that it was like looking through a very dense fog, yet I somehow made it home. This brings to mind another story which at the time was quite horrible, but looking back at it now, it just goes to show what a great sense of humor that God has.

My wife and my daughter were leaving state to go see my oldest daughter in Spokane, Washington. I was saying goodbye to them in the driveway when they left. I had to stay behind and work. Now I only see tunnel vision out of my left eye, so I did not see the pine bulbs on my left side. I walked straight into one of them, puncturing my cornea in my one good eye. I was at this time totally blind. I found my way to the front door and called the 911 who sent an ambulance. This is all within fifteen to twenty minutes after my wife and daughter had left for a week.

The doctors cleaned me up, and I had to wear a temp patch over my one working eye. Luckily, I had gone through mobility training through the blind commission. I took some sick time and vacation time from work for a week, but what was ironic about all of this was that when my wife and daughter got back a week later, I was almost healed up from my accident. So what I thought was going to be a one week of vacation ended up being one week on pain and misery. That's what I call ironic because I could not even drink with the antibiotics I was on. But looking on the bright side, I did get to keep my eye. So back to work I go.

I'm not quite sure how or why I survived through all that we went through. Back in 1990, right after I had lost most of my eyesight, I was still waiting to hear from Social Security and could not seem to find good reliable work anywhere. Luckily, we were on subsidized housing, or we would have really been in a bad spot. We were just married a year or so before and had moved into a little three-bedroom house in Oregon City, Oregon.

Not having any work made it very hard to supply the household needs along with my addiction. I got the opportunity to help a friend do his late night janitorial business, and with the three children being hungry, I took the job. At one of our clients, there was a brand-new bicycle that I saw as an opportunity to feed my children. So I took it and put it in the work vehicle without the other person knowing and continued doing my work. The next morning, when the friend I worked with dropped me off, I pulled out the bicycle from the back of the work vehicle. He asked where I got it. I told him that I had found it behind one of the businesses. Nothing more was ever said about it. But I knew the truth.

So later that day, I took the bike to a pawnshop and got $150 for it. I went straight home and then filled the house with food. I'm not so sure if I would have stolen the bike if I had not been high on methamphetamines. Anyway, the children were happy to be eating and all was good. At least until the next day when there was a knock on the front door. Of course, it was the police. I was arrested for a felony theft one and was taken to jail.

When I went to court, I explained to the judge the situation and said that if my children were hungry, I would do it again. I was not charged restitution because nothing was hurt or broken. The judge gave me eighteen months of supervised probation and told me that if I followed the rules, the charge would be lessened to a misdemeanor, and I could live my life normally from there. However, the problem was that I was not done drinking and doing drugs yet. What a fool I was.

In eighteen months, I had gone to jail multiple times for fighting, drinking, or using drugs. Sometimes all three. So my probation officer gave me a choice, go to drug treatment or go to prison. I picked drug treatment of course. They put me in jail a week before I had to go to Ontario, Oregon, but they let me out into the custody of my parents, long enough to get clean clothes, hygiene supplies, and cigarettes. It was also just long enough to get high and then off I went.

I actually learned a lot while I was there. But the hardest time I had was convincing the councilors that I was an abuser not an addict. They couldn't seem to quite get how it didn't bother me to be away from the drugs. It bothered me to be around drugs and not be able do them. That made me an abuser. I did learn that it was nice without them during those twenty-eight days. To anyone who felt they need to do drugs, I would absolutely tell them to try going to a program. I believe they are much needed in this ever-changing world of ours.

When I got back, I felt great for about an hour but then I felt a needle in my arm. My friends thought it would be nice to give me a welcome home gift, one, I think, I could have done without. Here is another thing for you who think that you have to do drugs to fit in or be a part of the crowd. Don't do it! Keep yourself as positive as possible. There is always a choice and when it comes down to it, it's only you who has to live with that choice that you have made, good or bad.

Back to the story. After getting back from drug treatment, almost every urine test from that point was dirty. I just couldn't figure out that all I had to do was not do it. By that time, I went to jail over thirty times, and quite frankly, the justice system had lost faith in me. I couldn't say as I blame them. Finally, my probation officer got tired of it and set up a little trap for me. When I saw my PO, he told me I was going to jail for a dirty UA for sixteen days. So the weekend before the hearing, I partied hard. When it came time for court, I had slept well the night before, got cleaned up, and tried to look presentable. Then the judge pulled a fast one on me. I was already going to jail for dirty urine but then he asked for a urine sample at the courthouse. I was done for.

The judge told me that if my urine came back clean, I would be released after sixteen days, but if it was dirty, I would be revoked sent to prison. I had been had. Sixteen days later, I was hauled away from court in tears, not because I knew what I had done wrong but because of the horrible position I had left my wife and children in. I vowed then I would never go back to that place, and I never did. I was sent to five prisons in four and a half months. Every day I wrote to my wife and reflected on the tasteless position I had left her in.

To this day, I have never forgiven myself for that, nor will I ever forget. But even in the darkest times, you can find light. I had no money except for $25—which my parents left on my books. One day as I was sitting in the light, I saw a man drawing a picture. I asked him if I could see it. He said yes reluctantly, and I flipped it over and started writing a poem from my heart. When I was done, we both were crying. He gave me the picture and asked if I could reprint the poem for his wife. I of course said yes, and this was where I found that my poetry could get me to my wife. I traded for all kinds of things but mostly writing supplies.

In 145 days, I sent my wife 145 letters and 148 poems all straight from my heart. I was a different man when I got out. I was twenty-six years old, going on twenty-seven. But the one thing I never forgot was exactly how I got there. Now you would think that after all of that, I would have stopped but that was not the case. Now I had a parole team—five guys to watch and keep track of me.

The first day I was out, we had to find a new place to live. The little bit of Social Security that I left for my wife was not nearly enough for her and three children to survive on. It did not take long for me to find a job though, and before long, we were sharing a place with some friends. As a matter of fact, my wife and I were living out of the back of a station wagon in front of her parents' house. The children were safe inside with my wife's parents, but we had to stay out in the car.

Meanwhile, we had applied for housing a year or so before, and it was finally our turn. The day before we moved, I had gotten high, stayed up all night, and was not really mentally okay. My wife had taken off, and at this point I was very suspicious. Even though I could barely see, I fired up the station wagon and went looking for her. I had to look out the driver's side window to follow the lines on the road. So when I crested a small hill, the sunshine hit me right in the eye. I did not see the car sitting there, waiting to turn left. By the time I saw her, it was too late, and I smacked into her. I backed up and asked if she was okay. She said yes, so I took off.

I was so scared that I drove straight to her parents' house, pulled all of the hub caps off, and threw them in the sticker bushes. Pretty bad, huh? The police showed up about an hour later, gave me a ticket for leaving the scene of the accident, along with failure to perform the duties of a driver. The police also told me that the young lady gave such a good description that they knew right where to find me. I did not go to jail though.

The next day my family and I moved to Canby, Oregon. But when we got to the parking lot, the transmission died. All we had was what we could fit in that old Ford Fairmont, and that was not a whole lot. So we got help from a local church who filled our apartment with food and furniture. We got the utilities turned on and got us completely settled in. Not long after we finished, there was a knock at the door, and it was my parole team. Apparently, they went door to door to find my apartment. So my parole officer looked at my wife and asked her if everything was okay. She replied to him that the fridge was full and the electricity was on and the rent was paid. He asked if there was anything else that she needed. She thought about it, and said no. My parole officer said good____.

I went to jail for ten days in medical confinement because my PO said after that little stunt, I was being grounded. It always seemed so easy because everywhere I went, I could find more work and find more drugs. Little did we know that by moving where we did, we were dropped right into the middle of a drug trafficking highway. There were drugs everywhere. Before I knew it, I was working 110 hours per week, which worked out to about $1,200 paychecks. That meant a lot of money to party on.

It only took about six months to get kicked out for excessive fighting and partying. They had to pay me back because I was six months ahead on rent. It was hard to try to fight because everywhere we turned was a dead end. Even on our way to court for the eviction notice, we were run into head-on, destroying our car and defaulted because we could not make it to the courthouse. At this point we had almost given up. I was finally off parole, and we decided that we were not going to give up no matter what.

So we moved again, this time to Portland, Oregon. We stayed in a few places, and I finally landed a good job with good benefits. I still drank and did drugs but somehow managed to make it to work. Even through homelessness, I still managed to make it to work.

Working during the night and sleeping where I could during the day was very hard on my body. Once or twice a month, I would rent us a motel room, sometimes to do drugs and drink, other times just to get some long needed rest. My children by then were grown up.

So luckily, my wife could stay with our daughter but their camper was too small for me to sleep there. After working all night, I would go get breakfast at St. Vincent De Paul's and would get a lunch to go to give to my wife. After spending all of winter outside, I finally got so sick that I had to be admitted into the hospital. I had walking pneumonia, and my feet were so raw that I could not walk anymore. It was at the end of the month when I was admitted, but I told them I did not get my Social Security until the second of the month. They agreed to let me stay as long as I promised to get a place to live.

The hospital let me out on the second. My wife and I walked and walked and walked until we came across a little apartment complex, went up, and talked to the manager and gave her $200 down on a one-bedroom apartment. She gave me the keys upon the promise that I would pay the rest when I got paid from my Job. She agreed and I signed the contract. My son and I slept in an empty apartment for the first night and the next day moved in. This was the last time that my family or I would ever be homeless again.

Time finally started to slow down. We did good in our little bedroom and before long I took on a second job. One day my wife and I were walking around the block and saw a townhouse for rent. A week later, we moved in. It was there that I changed my life forever. I was so sick of being high on my children's birthdays. I prayed for the strength to leave the drugs behind, and the next day, I no longer had drugs in my life. I have never done drugs since that moment.

At this point, I realized that I could overcome anything that was bad in my life by just asking for strength to stop, and that is how I have done it. No concealing, no drugs, no alcohol on meetings, no lectures or pills or anything else that modern day medicine has to offer. All that I needed was to ask God for strength and to believe in yourself and God.

That's all we have to do is believe. There were a lot of times when I thought that I might not make it, but I would ask myself if this was how I wanted to be remembered, not just by my family but by all of those whom I came into contact with. The answer was always I know that I am better than this. When that day came, on August 2, 2003, it was right before our youngest daughter's birthday, and as I looked in the mirror, I came to the realization that this was not who I am supposed to be. No longer did I ever went to be confused or unable to think straight. No more second-guessing my decisions of where to lead my life, as well as anyone else's.

It always starts with you and what you believe in. All of the rest will follow. Since the day I put that horrible life-destroying drug down, my life changed. When I woke up, I wanted to find a way to help people and gave them guidance away from the road that so many times tried to destroy my life and my family. From that day forward, my drive to succeed grew more and more every day, and along with that, my self-confidence, along with my faith, went through the roof.

So don't ever let anyone tell you that you can't do that because if this old blind man can do it, then you can do it too. As an example, after one year of being clean and sober, I got a call from a man that I worked for in between jobs. Once a week, he would come and get me on my day off, and he would drive me around to his different homes. I would mow the lawns, along with various other jobs. He would buy groceries for my family and I.

So when I came to my first anniversary away from the drugs and alcohol, he called me and said, "Hey! You know that house you have been taking care of for me in North Portland?"

I said, "Yes. I know the one …"

He then asked if I was still staying away from the drugs and alcohol, and I said yes. I had quit drinking on December 2, just four months after quitting the drugs.

He said, "Would you still like to live in that house?"

I said, "Of course, I would."

He then said, "Good. You will have to come and get the keys."

And I replied, "I already have a set."

Being the groundskeeper, I sometimes had to go to the bathroom.

He said, "Congratulations for being able to change my life around and for my family and I to move in."

I just fell into tears and said thank you to both Tom and God. After eleven years, I still lived there now. I wanted to tell you that because if I had never taken those steps into the unknown, I would not be where I am today. Thank you to all who kept believing in me right to the very end.

This is just one example of the miracles that still do happen in a world full of turmoil and doubt. There is always a choice in what we do, and in many cases, the choice that you decide to make affects more than just you. So please don't give up. There really is more out there for you. If you can dream it, then you can accomplish it. It doesn't matter if you are waiting tables, digging ditches, waving a sign, or working in a high-rise. This book is for those who are right on the edge, not knowing which way to turn or who to talk to. For those who have lost it all and are ready to pursue a new plan, this book will take care of you.

If you are one of those who feel that you can't live without the drugs, just ask yourself this. When all the pain comes rushing in and you can't find the drug that wouldn't cost you so much, I would like for you to try something different. Picture in your mind that drugs no longer exist but don't stop collecting money like they do. If you can make it three days or even a week, I want you to stop and empty out your pockets, count up all that you have saved, and go and buy yourself something that you've always wanted. I don't care if it is a week at a motel or a brand-new television like the one I bought.

Take the time to stop and look in the mirror and see if you remember a life where you were in control of both your thoughts and your finances. Could you get used to that person again, or maybe you never got the chance to be that person? I believe if you really enjoy having money and making your own choices, then all you have to do is tell yourself that you are tired of hurting and tired of giving up. What's yours is yours, no matter what that may be. You are worth it. You deserve to know what it's like to not be scared anymore.

The only vices that you have are the ones that you have chosen to carry with you. Each and every one of us are guilty of one thing or another, no exclusions. Even the rich and famous have baggage that they carry with them. I am here to tell you that the sooner you come to terms with what it is that has a hold of you, the safer and more relaxed you will be. I tell myself every morning that I can do it, that I am strong enough to take on whatever the world has to offer me. If I know you half as good as I know myself, you will come to realize that not everything the world offers up to you is good.

Now here is the real test: be happy within yourself, love yourself, and always try to give when you get the chance. Now I don't mean the guy at the bus stop who always asks you for change but never gets on the bus, but the person who doesn't have enough to buy their children food, or the person who needs help to cross the street. Do these type of things, and don't expect anything in return then watch the good person that smile back at you.

Sometimes you find a dollar on the ground. Other time it could be a new job opportunity or someone just noticing you for the first time and striking up a comfortable conversation. These are all good return on you, caring for someone other than yourself. Another added bonus is that after a while, you will feel your heart start to lighten and your soul start to smile.

I believe that this is how we are all supposed to live our lives. Yet we get caught up in what other people think that we should be who they think we should be. Personally, I love to teach, as well as learn, and the sooner we all begin doing this, the sooner all that stress will begin to leave your life. Just try it.

Chapter 7

Blindness and Relationships

So this chapter is about relationships and being blind. So it's been a tough challenge raising three kids starting at 17 years old going blind at 22 period when I first met my wife my heart dropped and I knew we were meant to be together and I was amazingly taken over by her beauty her blond hair and their blue eyes and her beautiful body and I instantly fell for her. But as time went on her beauty got better and it seemed like our relationship got worse as we started doing drugs and drinking and from that point on it just seemed to get worse and worse and worse until we stopped what we were doing in our 30s From there it got better but during this.

I don't know how she got the power and the ability. Just stay with me. No matter how bad I got and how ugly it got she always was there for me period So I'm trying to talk in this about relationships. So I was raised by my grandparents. I was adopted at four and a half months old.

I had three sets of grandparents my grandmother who and her husband Raymond Oliver. I was raised by my father was a long-haul truck driver. And from there it was a wonderful life until 14 years old.

We travel the United States every year we go to always the St. Louis Missouri where we had ever family on Grandpa side is life. And we always took a different way.

So I always got to see the wonderful site and it was a fantastic childhood. Even though I was Reckless and dangerous and out of hand, I always period but through that I learn to be respectful and learn to have good values and was ready for a family at 17. so I thought period I had no idea what it would entail when I have three children under our wings and what it entailed to take care of them and to raise them. It was a whole new world to me, but I was excited for it because I had a wonderful wife and I have wonderful children and they all grew up to be very good and very Successful, which I'm so proud of but we definitely had our bad times.

We were homeless for nine and a half months on a riverbank and I was working two full-time jobs, but we had three final eviction decrees and nobody would rent to us but through the power of ability to speak with people.

I managed to find us a little one-bedroom apartment. Mint and we ended up staying there and have never been homeless since and it just the power of ability to be positive and keep moving forward and never giving up that got us through that and believing in God and doing a lot of prayers. I'll tell you in that at times. And absolute hell at other times and I always thought it was because they were doing something wrong or somebody else was doing something wrong and coming to find out it wasn't it was me and everything that I was doing was incorrect.

I thought it was good, but I was gone 20 hours a day and away from my family working. And it ended up I was growing apart from my family instead of go out growing closer to them and that get a lot of damage. JH and I don't know that they'll ever forgive me for that, but I keep asking for it and I know that God has forgiven me, but it's a lot different than people forgiving than God.

I just wanted to say that if you're having problems with your relationships pray about it and look in the mirror and see if there's something that you may be doing wrong. There may be nothing you're doing wrong or it could be the littlest thing but in relationships you need to make sure that it's a mutual agreement. It's always a job.

It's something that you can't quit and you can't walk away from it something that you need to make sure that you're both willing to take on whatever it takes and do whatever it takes to make your family work and stay together, but that also means being there with him as well where I was not being gone. As long as I was working as hard as I was being taught that you know working is what you do to support your family.

I did that and did All the time, especially after I quit drinking and doing drugs, I threw myself into work and I'm afraid a lot of people do that as a recourse if they're quitting something as powerful as drugs or alcohol and in return you're moving away from your family instead of towards them because you're never there to protect them give them supports or give them positive input and that's what happened to me.

So I just want to share with other people that it's okay to stay positive and and be confident but also don't overwork yourself and invest the time in your family as much as you can because in the end that means everything so it's just a short chapter about relationships and my input and trying to say don't do what I did.

It's good to work, but don't work too much and it's good to have fun, but don't have too much fun. But make sure you always have love in your heart and towards your family and the people around you because when you lose them, it's too late. anyway, that is the end of this chapter once again, pray about it believe and got stay positive and look forward to New Beginnings as we all continue to motivate forward and become stronger people as we get older and hindsight is 20/20 is what they say look to the past to learn from not to hold grudges and look to the Future to be positive and move forward towards it but live in the present and do the best that you can and give the best love that you can and the best advice that you can and be the best that you can be the end.

Chapter 8

Finding My Inspiration and Strength

IF WE ALL LOOK deep within ourselves, what you should find is a hunger to better ourselves. Ask the closest person to you. Be it a friend or a spouse or even a close family member, and ask them just exactly what it is that pulls them toward you. This probably will vary according to whom it is you talk to. Think long and hard about the answers that you receive. This should be the basis of where to find more inspiration than just what you think and feel.

    I personally have found that the more I look back and remember all of those people in my life that took the time to teach me some lessons in life and living, the easier it is to find the strength that I need to keep me going every day. As long as I was learning something, then I was still paying tribute to the time and effort that they spent on me. There is no price that can be put on that time. I would like to believe that most of us are being taught right from wrong at a very young age. It is only how well that we can carry this forward, which will help to shape the future of our world and what it will become. We have all done wrong. There is no escaping from it because if we don't make mistakes, we just don't seem to learn what not to do as well.

Every time that I would feel down or like I could not go on, I would remember that there's always somebody worse than I was, yet they could still function and accomplish that which would seem impossible to most people. I took a long time for me to figure out that all it took was belief in myself and in those who chose to show me that it was always possible. It may surprise you to know that the name patches stitched onto our country's armed forces, as well as the coastguard, is all done by people that are totally blind.

I had the fine enjoyment to be able to work with these fine men and women twice. The first time I worked with them was in a back room in the back of a Bingo Hall in Northeast Portland. I was working from 6:00 a.m. to 2:00 p.m. at a major chain grocery store and then at the Bingo Hall from 3:00 p.m. to 11:00 p.m., five days a week. Then I would walk six-and-a-half miles from the mall to my house in Oregon City every night. It was too late for me to ride the bus, so I had to walk. I refused to quit one of the jobs not because I was a glutton for punishment but because I had a wife and three children, along with a brand-new grandchild at home, depending on me to keep a roof over their heads.

Every time I would start to feel down, I would either think about them, or I would think about the other people that I was working with. This was because not only were they totally blind but I had seen for myself them _____, take apart, and reassemble those industrial sewing machines, which personally, I don't think that not a single-sighted person could do what they were doing. Plus, they would not allow anyone looking or not near those machines. They personally took the time to show and teach me some of their trade secrets using only their minds and their fingers.

If you were to watch this, you would draw inspiration from it too. Every painstaking step that I took, I became more and more thankful for what God had given to me and what he had allowed me to experience every day. There were several times that I would wake up with the sun coming up, telling me it was time to do it again. I would be on the front steps of my apartment, usually with a 40 oz of beer between my legs that was always untouched. I would buy it on the way home, thinking I would get to enjoy it when I got home. I never did get to, not even once.

I was able to finally let go because I had become sick with double walking pneumonia from walking home in the cold and the rain. The company moved from the back of the Bingo Hall, and I went back to work for them about fifteen years later. There were a couple of extra problems though. When I tried going back to work for them, I was working two other jobs, but that was not the main problem. The main problem was that after all of the years of hard labor, the neuropathy caused by my diabetes had taken the feeling from the tips of my fingers, so I could not thread the needles even with the needle threaders.

I really wanted that job to work because of the respect that I had from the bottom of my heart for those men and women. Even the blind took the time to show me how to see with my mind and body. It truly is hard to explain unless you have experienced it for yourself. To all the people out there who read my book, do me and yourself a favor. Go out and do something nice for someone else at least once a day. I guarantee it will make your heart and soul to its very deepest points.

I can remember this one time when I was at work for a construction company where I was the laborer foreman. I was helping the framers stand up a wall on the third floor when my friend, Bear, got stung by a _____ and it just so happened that he was deathly allergic to them. The man was probably 6'2" tall and weighed at least 250 pounds. No one else could carry him, so I threw him over my shoulder and went down two tall ladders with him on my back. He was already unconscious by the time that I got him on the ground.

There was already a car waiting for him at the bottom. He made it to the hospital with five minutes to spare. After I found out he was going to be okay, I couldn't get the smile off of my face and the feeling out of my heart. Sometimes, it's simple deeds and other times, someone's life could be dependent upon it. Either way, you should never feel bad for helping others out. I also am a true believer that karma is alive. This means that if you do a good deed, it always comes back to you even though a lot of times, people don't even recognize what has been given to them.

Somewhere people got stuck on thinking that doing good deeds means that you will get money or a better job or even a win or the lottery. Though those things could be nice, it should be the simple things that we watch out for. Someone giving you a nice gesture or someone saying, "Hey! You dropped your wallet or purse. Karma does not always mean profit. Look for the nice things that make you smile. It is not hard to make an effort to be nice to someone. I'm sure that we are all guilty of someone dropping something, and we just walk on by because we are all so caught up in our own bubble, too selfish to notice the person in need.

No matter what is going on in our lives, we cannot afford to lose our humanity. I used to be really mean when I was younger and trust me, I have paid for those faults in one way or another. That was until I found that the more helpful and nice I was, the better my life got. We need to trust that God wants us to treat each other better. Look at what is going on in the world today. With all of the racism, violence, and death, if everyone was to actually care about what was going on around each and every one of us, the world would change pretty much instantly. Yet the small number of people that really live like that every day are being trampled over by those people after the almighty dollar. How sickeningly sad is that?

It goes to show me that what my parents were going through, talking about when it came to the world as they would say it, "Hell in a hand basket," is what seems to be going on right in front of all of us. When my parents set me and my sister down and said that as we get older, the faster the years go by. Of course, at that time, it made no sense to us. But now as I grow older, and am definitely less able to keep up with my time, let alone myself, I realize what it was that they meant by that statement.

Stay Focused

Obviously, we slow down with age and the work still just keeps on going round and round.

I have now become one of those people who yell, "Turn it down!" or "Slow Down!" I can actually remember laughing to myself, saying, "I will never be that guy," and "If it's too loud, then your too old."

Concerts enthused me and now they frustrate me. Somewhere along the way, I have turned into that *guy*.

I tried something that I haven't tried in a long time. I have become more and more tired as the days went on while I was not working because of my injury. And actually, it's not that I couldn't work. It's that I have not found work yet. Back to the trick of curing tiredness. I went outside during a light sprinkle, and I started walking as fast as I could, up and down the street twice.

By the time I was done, my heart was pumping and my pulse was racing. After sitting down for ten minutes, I felt wide awake. I believe that no matter how old you get, if you are able to do this simple activity, then you can overcome your fatigue. I do, however, fall into my human side, just like anyone else. It is easy to get sidetracked from our own goals and go astray. As an example, I misplaced my glasses five days ago, so I was unable to work on my book properly.

Instead of looking for them myself, I kept asking everyone else to, "Let me know if they see them." I finally got up and found them myself. All it took was a little effort.

If you want to receive success, then you have to work your buns off for it. I don't recall ever making it anywhere without having to prove that I was the one that they just could not do without. There are a few and only a few ways to do that. One is by convincing them that you know more than anyone else or at least as much but visually impaired. I have always had to be sneaky and smart. The next thing you need to do when you are physically challenged is to work twice as hard just to seem like you are as normal as anyone else.

Almost every person or company I have ever worked for or I had convinced that I was a klutz. That generally worked until I had talked too much or made a mistake, and them finding out that I was blind, diabetic, or both. Next is remembering everything that you are shown or taught the first time, so that you don't have to ask a whole lot of questions and believe it.

Employers enjoy not having to repeat themselves. Sometimes, you can keep a job going just by flying below the radar. However, something I said about questions, when you have been hired, make sure that you ask all the questions at that time, and you have to take notes. You would not believe how much it can really help to have something to refer back to.

The next thing that you want to do is be very confident in yourself. If you don't have a doubt in your abilities, then odds are the person hiring you won't either. Confidence has always been a very strong key in landing a job. Believe in yourself because sometimes, you are the only one who will. I have gotten more jobs that people told me I couldn't than the ones who told me I could. Knowledge is everything when it comes to proving you can do what you say. And if you don't know what you're doing then you have a choice—lie and figure it out or don't take the job. I personally don't recall ever turning down work of any kind.

Some of these are choices that most people take for granted because they don't have to think about whether or not they are strong enough or smart enough or even healthy enough to function just as efficient as everyone else does.

So if you are not able to physically keep up, then mentally leave them all behind. You don't have to be the strongest or the fastest if you can shine from the inside out. This is no joke. It really does work if you are able to work it and make it work for you. Self-motivation is a beautiful thing especially if you have those around you, convincing you that there is nothing you cannot do. Don't show fear, and don't hesitate. There is a reason for the saying, "He who hesitates is lost." Follow your instincts because believe it or not, that is sometimes all that some have to go on.

Everyone has to start out knowing what to do or what to say. It takes practice but if you work hard at it, you will lead the pack. You don't have to be a natural-born leader to convince others that you know what you're doing. If you pay attention and watch closely, you will learn without having to say or ask anything. As I go through life, it seems that the more people that I meet, the more I am reminded of the power of the human spirit. I have heard people say that people don't change but then have the pleasure of watching them change themselves.

The strength that others muster up just to keep going or just to keep their families fed and housed is for some beyond comprehension and for others just day to day living. Each and every one of them though manage to survive another day, so they can get up and do it again the next. And to all of those who are trying something new, whether it be school or a new job, I tip my hat and bow in recognition to all that you try and do. If we don't further ourselves and learn new things, then we become stagnant. The longer that you don't do something, the more that you don't want to do anything.

I myself like to start off with a dream, make a goal, and then go for it. I put off writing this book for almost ten years, but it kept eating at me. When I had my accident at work, I found myself wondering what to do; being stuck at home but then remember what it was that I told others to do. I bought a notebook, worked past the fears of failure, and started writing. Now I am getting ready to publish my book in hopes that I can share it with the world. Don't ever look at anything as one dimension or impossible. If there is a will, there is always a way to make it work. If it was easy, then everyone would do it. The impossible is only until someone does it.

A lot of people can type a book out, but I chose to handwrite mine.

After the age of the computer, it seems that people forgot how to do it in a traditional form. I'm here to tell you, learn how to read and write and all of those other things that people consider to be knowledge. It really is a good thing to know. Go out and follow your own dreams, meet people, and don't see in colors. It really does not make sense. All of the prejudice in the world, from what I have experienced, most of the people met just want to get along and strive to get along.

I am writing this book in hopes to let the world know that it doesn't matter what kind of challenges you may have because if you want to succeed bad enough, we, as people, will always find a way to enable ourselves to succeed at something. Try new things and find what you are good at. Enjoy what you do. It is a very important part of being successful. If you really enjoy what you are doing, you are less apt to become bored at it. I did the same job for thirteen-and-a-half years and never got bored.

There is a secret to doing this, and I will let you know what it is. Try to remember all of the positive things and forget the negative. Release all the ghosts in your closet, and you will be amazed at the relief that you will feel almost immediately. Bad memories cause anxiety and stress, and it can cause you to be very short-tempered and angry. You want people to want to be around you. When you are happy and stress-free, people become curious as to why. Be honest with yourself. Being dishonest is like digging a hole that never gets filled in. This also causes stress.

Make learning fun. I learned a long time ago that if you make games up while you learn, the more apt you are to remember. Games relieve stress and anxiety. The more fun you have, the more you learn, and the smarter you get. Try to listen to what people try to teach you. Listen first, and then it is up to you from that point, whether or not to discard the information.

Be safe. Take the time to learn the safest way to do anything that you try. Better safe than sorry.

Never make excuses. Learn from your mistakes and grow from them. Nobody likes a whiner or someone who tries to get out of trouble by making some sort of excuse. The people around you will tend to respect you more if you admit to your mistakes, and then ask questions on how to perform the task the right away.

Stay confident. Be ready for anything, and the odds are you will be picked out of a crowd to perform new tasks, which will not only build your confidence but the companies as well.

Be the first to volunteer. Companies are looking for the person to lean their crews.

Be assertive but not overbearing. Remember, you want people to want to work with you.

Leave your problems at home. I know it is sometimes hard, but nobody wants to hear about it unless it's positive.

Don't get cocky. Unless you are obligated to a contract, it does not take much for a company to let you go if they want to. Don't ever think that you can't be replaced because there are dozens of others that will and can do more for less. So be thankful for what you have, and don't be pushy.

Stay clean. Hygiene is everything when it comes to working with other people. It lets them know that you care about yourself, as well as others. Nobody likes a stinky or unclean person. If you have, carry some deodorant, toothbrush and toothpaste, and a clean change of clothes with you.

Always be at least fifteen minutes early. All it takes is one tardy, and you could miss out on a promotion or a raise. It really is worth it to always be early. Plus, the company will come to depend on you as punctual and reliable person. This is a good thing.

Always have a backup plan. A lot of things can happen out there, so plan out at least two or three other ways or options for how to get there, be it a cab or bicycle or car or on foot.

Always be prepared for anything. Stuff happens, companies downsize, and layoffs happen. Keep your chin up, and never give them a reason to look your way.

Always look the employer straight in the eye. Show them that you are paying attention, not mentally wondering off to someplace else. Be sure and shake their hand and thank them for their time. Sometimes that alone is enough to get you the job or promotion. They expect respect, so give it to them. It will go a long way.

Be a team player. Always be ready to help when you can and where you can. Continue to be as helpful as possible, so that when the chips are down, they will know they can count on you.

Wear the proper attire. Dress appropriately. Don't show up to work construction in a suit or to an office wearing a tool belt or T-shirt and jeans. Sometimes some companies have what's called a casual Friday, but generally, there is a certain dress code, so follow it!

If you get injured on the job, make a report first thing. Companies will usually ask you to go to the hospital to give a urinalysis and get checked out. Make sure that it is clean and clear, or it could affect your claim. Take pictures. This can be very helpful when it comes to explaining the extent of your injuries. Keep a daily journal as well, so that you will have something to refer back for.

As a completion to this book, I will leave you with this note: If you believe that you can do something, then don't ever let anyone say to you that you can't. Start off slow, and remember that very rarely does or is a person good at something the first time. So don't give up because there usually will be many failed attempts long before there are successful ones. Keep trying and be positive toward yourself and the others around you. Good luck, and I hope you have a wonderful life.

I move from the middle of the hill and Oregon City, Oregon to the top of the hill Hilltop in Oregon City, Oregon and I was rollerskating Outdoors full-time and I was introduced to marijuana at 15 years old and that's when I started smoking pot, and from there I continued doing that while I went through college and met good friends Norman David Willie and I was introduced to do some other things like mushrooms and methamphetamines and I was right before my 18th birthday.

I did my first line of methamphetamines and it was all fun and and good than that. At that time and the next day, I introduce my girlfriend to it and gave her a line of methamphetamines. And that was the beginning of the end from there.

We have fun for a couple three years, you know, we do it once in awhile recreationally and damn it started to become a problem. And by the time I was 22, I Well, I'm doing it on a regular basis and the difference was I was an abused or not an addict.

So the difference there was once I had it I had to do it all but if I did without it I was fine period it sounds like me. So from there, I lost my eyes at 22 years old. I was driving and riding motorcycle up until then, but from there at once I lost my eyes. I started losing them at 18 years old and they progressively got worse more surgeries after 15 major eye surgeries. I can no longer see out of my right eye and only tunnel vision out of my left eye. And so I was unable to work for six months as I file for disability. And once I got my disability I found out that I could still work.

So being raised by my grandparents at a young age. I had third values and the values were that I take care of my family no matter what so I started working odds and in jobs worked for several paper companies work doing digging ditches building fences construction, whatever I could find to do that. Was what I get as long as it made money for the family well during this time. Of course, I was doing drugs and staying up for two to three days now for a lot of people. That would be okay. I guess if you did that kind of drug, but for me after two days, it was like looking through a waving Fishbowl and I don't know how to really describe it but it was hard to function and see but somehow I managed with the help of God walking by my side who at that time. I'm guessing didn't pay too much attention to me considering what I was doing to myself.

My body but I still kept the faith and kept going kept trudging had horrible accidents had horrible things happen to you. Sorry. Scratch that last bit because my brother and I apologize. Anyway, so I continued working my eyes continued getting worse. And at this point now I will discuss that more and blind luck to one foot in the grave. But right now I am discussing about up until 2015 when I wrote this book. I was in a wheelchair with half my right foot gone.

You do an accident at work where I was a general manager and running 11 stores with 37 employees period until I got hurt at work. but I when I kept doing drugs, I went blind right after I got married at 22 years old.

We have three small children and it was endowed into me to do whatever it took to take care of my family. And so that's what I did no matter what and through that. I learned a lot got drunk and I a lot got in a lot of fights and The worst damage that I ever did was to my family. Period it was hard for all this because all I wanted to do was work because that's all I knew to do to take care of my family.

But at the same time it was destroying my family one because I was gone all the time and to because when I was home, we were either fighting or loving there was no in between. And that made it really hard to survive especially for the children they grew up strong and I'm really proud of them, but it was a broken family to start with and because of the drugs and alcohol and if you're out there doing them, all I want to say is don't do it because it really does not help you may think it's helping you you may think it feels great, but it's destroying you and the people around you. So in short, I just want to say that through my experiences with all of this for 17 years. I went through 1.4 million dollars in drugs and alcohol and ended up with nothing. But in 2003, I woke up one day. And I thought what am I doing? It's my daughter's 16th birthday coming up and I'm high and I did not feel comfortable doing that. So I prayed about it the night before and I woke up and it was gone for my life. And that was August 4th of 2003 and in October of 2003. I quit drinking. And life was amazingly better. I always thought it was everybody else. That was the problem. But once I quit I realized that I really was the problem and until I stopped.

I never realized that period So I'm just trying to convey this to the rest of the world that if you're thinking about doing drugs or his me that life's not good enough for you and it's pushing you that way don't do it. There's Heather ways of getting around it. Try praying to Jesus Christ or God or your higher power.

Whoever that may be and ask for deliverance and help from these thoughts and these feelings and what you're doing. and you'll find that you'll have the strength to do it. So in that I just wanted to say I have tons of stories, but I don't want to eat up this book with all of them and you guys hearing all that.

I'll talk more about that in my second book. But right now my main message to convey is please stay away from drugs and alcohol. It's not helping you or the people around you. It's destroying you. And the people around you and if you have a family it's the worst thing in the world you could ever do period So that probably will be the end of this chapter until the next book and I will talk more about it. But for now stay safe.

God bless you and good luck be positive. Keep your eyes to the Horizon and make sure you're always moving forward never doubt yourself always believe in yourself, and you'll always do better and other people will realize that in That in you an wonder what keeps you so positive and they will ask and tell them exactly what it is that keeps you positive and gives you strength. I know it did me and I'm still going no matter what and staying positive and accomplishing amazing things. The end are.

About the Author

IMAGINE BEING TWENTY-TWO YEARS old, having a good job, a driver's license with a nice car, being newly wed to a beautiful lady with three wonderful children.

Everything was perfect. Then one day, there was a loud pop in my eye, and everything started to turn red. This was the end of my life as I knew it. I have been a type 1 diabetic (dependent on insulin) since I was five and had been warned of what was going to happen if I did not take care of myself properly. Losing my sight was just the beginning of a long road of learning by trial and error.

This is a book about the true-life struggles of a legally blind man trying to raise a family while fighting drug addiction, alcoholism, and ADHD. But I only knew one thing, and that was to fight for what I believe in.

Being dropped into a hole of desperation with what seems to be no hope can lead to amazing things. I prayed for strength as I learned to figure out just what it takes to be successful in a sight-driven world. This is no easy task by any means. Try doing it with your eyes closed.

I needed to learn to overcome the fear and break through the obstacles to teach others that it does not matter what your challenge in life is because if you put your mind to it, and you really want it, there is nothing that the human spirit cannot overcome. You have to keep trying. Even if you fail, get up and do it again until you get it right.

I hope that this book can help people understand that if you have the will, you do have the ability to achieve great things.

It does not matter what other people say to you. It matters what you say to yourself.

You can do it, and don't ever believe anybody who says you can't.

My motto has always been, "If a blind guy can do it, then anybody can." There are others out in the world every day proving it, so get up and be the one who gets it done.

Believe in yourself because sometimes no one else will.

There is always someone there to back you up, even if it is only God. You can find the strength you're after if you just believe.

I have been on the bottom and worked my way to the top more than once. So join me as I share some of my experiences with you.

Remember, you are special too. So prove it, and *be that person* you are meant to be.

Welcome to my life.

www.ingramcontent.com/pod-product-compliance
Lightning Source LLC
Chambersburg PA
CBHW020309010526
44107CB00001B/39